Loving Them Back

Leading Them Home

To order additional copies of *Loving Them Back, Leading Them Home*
by Barry Gane, call 1-800-765-6955.
Visit us at **www.reviewandherald.com** for information on other
Review and Herald® products.

Any church is only

one generation away

from extinction

Loving Them Back Leading Them Home

Barry Gane, Ph.D.

REVIEW AND HERALD® PUBLISHING ASSOCIATION

Since 1861 | www.reviewandherald.com

Published by Review and Herald® Publishing Association, Hagerstown, MD 21741-1119

Review and Herald® titles may be purchased in bulk for educational, business, fund-raising, or sales promotional use. For information, e-mail SpecialMarkets@reviewandherald.com.

The Review and Herald® Publishing Association publishes biblically based materials for spiritual, physical, and mental growth and Christian discipleship.

The author assumes full responsibility for the accuracy of all facts and quotations as cited in this book.

This book was
Edited by Steven S. Winn
Copyedited by James Hoffer
Cover designed by Trent Truman
Interior designed by Tina M. Ivany
Cover art by ©istockphoto.com/iFry
Typeset: Bembo 11/14

PRINTED IN U.S.A.

14 13 12 11 10   5 4 3 2 1

Library of Congress Cataloging-in-Publication Data
Gane, Barry, 1950-   .
  Loving them back, leading them home / Barry Gane.
      p. cm.
1. Church work with youth. 2. Missions. 3. Evangelistic work. I. Title.
  BV4447.G357 2010
  259'.23—dc22

                              2009037312

ISBN 978-0-8280-2378-8

Contents

Chapter 1

Coming Home

I owe my connection with the church to the unconditional love of godly Christian parents and to a church family who saw potential in me—a potential that only God could have revealed.

Just after my seventeenth birthday I finally made the decision to be baptized. I hoped that the anger, questioning, and disquiet would be washed away in the baptismal water—that I would be changed. I was disappointed to find that the black gown and ceremony had changed nothing, and especially not me. In the following weeks I became further enmeshed with a group of friends I thought I had left behind. But instead of my interest fading away, the bike gang seemed to hold even greater appeal. With my last years of high school still ahead of me, I decided to spend less and less time there and more and more time with the bikers. I left home regularly, telling my parents that I would never return. Instead of acting with the anger I expected, they simply let me know that their door was always open.

I was totally self-centered, angry with everyone without a reason—one of those obnoxious kids. Apart from myself, only one person really mattered to me, my girlfriend. But even she could not calm the storm inside me, so I broke up with her and started a completely new life in another state. With just a few dollars in my pocket, a change of clothes, a sleeping bag, and an attitude that said, "anywhere is better than here," I headed west to a new life. A couple of friends who felt the same way joined me for the adventure.

Tired of sleeping on the ground and as hungry as horses, we limped into Adelaide, 1,200 miles from home. One of the guys tried to contact some friends, only to find that they were away. We decided to visit anyway; it was an easy house to break into. We thought we'd stay until they came home or until one of the neighbors called the police. But nothing happened, maybe because the owner of the house was a pastor and the neighbors were used to seeing kids around.

We ate the food in the fridge but couldn't bring ourselves to sleep in the family's beds. After a few days of sleeping on the floor I was ready to try something different. Stumbling over an old mattress in the backyard, I dragged it inside. It smelled a bit, but at least it would be softer than the floor. When we returned to the house in the early hours of the next morning, I rolled out my sleeping bag on the mattress and fell into an exhausted sleep. When I awoke, I was covered in fleas. With bites all over me, I was scratching the skin off my body. There were so many fleas that the floor seemed to move.

Home started to look pretty good and I decided that it was time to head back. When I finally dragged myself back to my parents' house, I had hitch-hiked for 48 hours and was struggling with a severe case of the flu. I was exhausted and hadn't eaten well for a couple of weeks. Ignoring my need for sleep, the first thing I did was to call my girlfriend and ask her whether she'd go out for the night.

"I thought you were never coming back," she questioned.

"Well, I'm here. Do you want to go out or not?"

She agreed. I asked dad for a loan of the pickup and some cash and headed off to pick up my girl. We drove down to a deserted beach and spent hours catching up. Finally, in the early hours of the morning we headed for home. With sand still jumping off the truck tires from the beach I discovered we were nearly out of gas. After filling the tank at a gas station I felt my pocket for my wallet. Nothing. Thinking it must have fallen down behind the seat, I groped around the truck's interior. Still nothing. Swinging open the glass door, I walked up to the cashier and informed him that I'd lost my wallet.

"I hear that story every night. Pull the other leg—it whistles! You stay right there. I'm calling the police," he announced.

My exhausted brain jumped into action. I would punch his lights out, make a run for it, and hope that I could race the pickup out of sight before he could take down the license plate number. Then sanity prevailed. I simply asked, "Why don't you phone my dad?"

With his ear to the phone and his eye on me, he finally gave in to my father's promise to pay for the gas. Before he could hang up, I grabbed the receiver and spoke to my dad with uncharacteristic consideration: "Dad, go to bed. Don't wait up for me. I'm coming home, but I just want to go down to the beach to try to find my wallet."

As I walked away, the cashier shot out, "He seems like a decent man— don't know where he got you!"

Turning the key in the truck's ignition, I rushed off a simple, unholy prayer. "God, I want the wallet, all right?" There was no "Dear Father" or "Amen," just a rattled demand—more of a curse than a prayer. Back at the beach we retraced our steps at the place where we'd spent most of our time. Combing my fingers through the sand, it wasn't long before they unearthed my wallet. A stroke of good luck!

Driving toward home, I found myself teetering on the brink of sleep. Mesmerized by the speedometer, I caught myself drifting toward the curb several times. I begged my girlfriend to talk to me, but she was almost as exhausted as I was. Sprawled across the front seat, her head on my lap, she quickly drifted into a deep sleep. I turned the radio up, rolled down the window, sang at the top of my lungs, and continued driving. My body finally shut down, and I gave in to sleep's irresistible invitation.

BANG! My eyes flew open and I was welcomed back to consciousness by sparks dancing across the hood of the truck. I looked down and saw that my girlfriend was drenched in blood. The engine had come right through the firewall and appeared to have married itself to her body. My hands flew to each door handle, but neither door would budge. Leaning back, I crawled on top of her and kicked and kicked until her window exploded. Wriggling through her window, I fell onto the road. I struggled to my feet, reached through the jagged opening of her window, grabbed her by the legs, and pulled her out of the truck and as far away from the crash site as possible.

People began streaming from their darkened homes, flashlights crisscrossing the accident scene. I had struck a power pole, knocking out the electricity for the entire area. As I lay there on the ground, blood pumping from my head, arms, and knee, I realized that my girlfriend had not moved or breathed since I had pulled her from the pickup. In desperation I yelled, "Is Karen* all right? Is she all right?" I was assured that she was fine. Some people carried me away from the accident scene, propped me against a tree, and told me to press my thumb to the side of my head and to put pressure on my knee to stop the bleeding, as arteries were severed in both places. As I watched, someone brought out a blanket, unfolded it, and completely covered the still form of my girlfriend.

I began to pray for a second time that night—a prayer of absolute desperation. This time it began in the traditional way: "Dear God . . ." The cold realization flooded over me that I had killed the only person I really cared about. In despair I began to plead with God, but nothing happened. The ambulance arrived and the attendants loaded Karen into it, sitting me down beside her. In the darkness of the jostling ride to the hospital, my prayer increased in intensity. "Dear God, if You'll do this, then You can have me." What a great deal I was offering God! Looking back, I can hardly believe that He would even have been interested. At the end of my prayer, however, I heard a shrill, bloodcurdling scream, the type that only girls can make. It made my hair stand on end, but it was beautiful. Although Karen didn't regain consciousness at that moment, I knew she was alive. I exhaled another prayer: "Thanks, Lord."

When we got to the hospital, they began to strip away my clothing and shave the hair from the side of my head. I had nearly lost an ear and my leg was badly damaged. Just before they began the repair work, my father walked in. I wondered who told him where to find me. He asked whether Karen and I were going to be all right, and the surgeons assured him that there seemed to be no life-threatening damage, although the girl was still unconscious. And then, much to my embarrassment, he asked if he could pray. Just below the surface of my chagrin was the sense that something was changing inside me.

It was not until later that I found out the rest of that night's story. My father normally wouldn't go to sleep until I was home, which meant many sleepless hours. But this night he *had* gone to sleep. Jolted awake just after 2 a.m., he got down on his knees and prayed a second time that night for his boy who was out there somewhere. Flipping the light switch, but with no change in the darkened room, he realized the electricity had gone out. He walked to the kitchen and saw the electric clock flashing the time of the power disruption. He had been jolted awake at the precise moment I had hit the pole.

Shaking my mother awake, they headed off together to find their boy. He slowed as he passed his pickup wrapped around the power pole just 10 miles from home. Seeing no one at the scene, he drove straight to the hospital, arriving shortly after I did.

Within a few weeks, my girlfriend had mostly recovered, with just minor scarring, and I was released soon after she was. The experience made a profoundly positive impact on my mind, but I had not yet submitted to Jesus as my Savior, and I was certainly not back at church. There was still a long way to go.

One Sabbath after I had returned home, the family left for church, leaving me an invitation to join them. As I crawled under an old wreck of a car I was repairing, it dawned on me that I hadn't fulfilled my promise: "God, if you'll do this, You can have me." Suddenly I was back in that ambulance, huddled next to my unconscious and bleeding girlfriend. God had come through on His end of the bargain, and I was overwhelmed with a sense that now it was my turn.

It seemed obvious to me that the first step would be to go back to church. But with anger still simmering inside me, I didn't really want to go, and so I hatched a plan that would ensure the church's rejection of me. Unwashed, clad in my leathers, and my hair and hands streaked with black grease, I swung my leg over my motorcycle and roared off to church. I did a couple of wheelies in the parking lot, and followed them up with a few donuts, spraying dirt in every direction. I wanted them to know that I'd arrived.

I sauntered into the sanctuary, slumped into an empty pew at the back, and looked to the front, waiting for the looks of despising horror to register on the faces of the congregation. Instead I saw tears rolling down my father's cheeks as he sat on the platform next to the preacher. I expected the head deacon, who had two perfect children—one in college training for the ministry and the other about to marry a church worker—to come over, berate me in a loud voice, and command me to leave. You should know better! Your father is the elder! What are you doing in church dressed like that?

With a heart simmering with bile, I had a mouth full of venom ready and waiting to spew all over him. Then I would walk out of the church and say, See, I tried, but they didn't want me, God. But the deacon didn't come.

The sermon dragged on and on. At long last, the closing hymn marked the end of the agony, and the congregation began to filter toward the door at the back. As they passed my pew, there were no despising glances, no horror-filled expressions, just reassuring hands on my shoulders and sincere comments about how good it was to see me at church. This wasn't what I expected, nor what I wanted.

Following the line of people exiting the sanctuary, I saw my dad at his post, shaking hands with each person. As I extended my hand to him, he swallowed hard. He said nothing, but the handshake spoke volumes. Then I placed my greasy hand in the hand of the pastor, and I could see the start of the reaction I had wanted. But he bit his tongue and said nothing.

Walking down the steps at the front of the church, I saw the deacon approaching with his eye on me. He's kept it until now, I thought. I was sure that he was going to hit me, so I decided to slug him first and then run like mad, hoping that my motorcycle would start before the rest of the deacons got to me. But instead of a closed fist, he reached out with an open hand. As he pumped my arm, he told me how thrilled he was that I was back at church. No sooner had he let go of my hand than a little man who stood only as high as my chin threw his arms around me and began to weep on my shoulder. "Welcome home," he gushed, assuring me of his prayers and how he had longed for the day that I would come back.

Standing there on the steps of that church, 19 years old, I felt awkward, embarrassed, but strangely warm. That was my first day back at church, and I have never missed since. It took a while for God to change my exterior, but His Spirit had already begun to work powerfully on the inside.

Looking back over my childhood and adolescence, I have asked myself what it was that moved me from anger and alienation to a realization and acceptance of God's love for me personally. I had godly parents who did not deserve to have a son like me but who consistently and unconditionally accepted me. I went to a Christian school where teachers let me know how much they cared for me. With these integral factors as background, it was the unconditional love and support of a church who were a true family to me, a family who really understood community and acceptance, that finally broke through my shell and helped me realize how important I was in the eyes of God.

In the years since I have seen my experience echoed in the lives of young people over and over, and I believe with all my heart that the positive ending of my story means hope for kids going through the same process. Having been away from the church, I know how great it is to be home. I have a passion for that restless kid running from home, that angry kid seething with alienation, that leather-clad kid at the back of the church expecting rejection. I long for him to come home, for her to be restored, for them to be reconnected to the church family, and to know just how good it can be.

---

* This is not her real name. I have changed the names throughout the book to protect anonymity.

Chapter 2

Youth, the Church of Today

Every church is only one generation away from extinction. The youth of the church are its greatest asset and hope. So often, when youth "get serious" about their faith, they bring to the church a contagious enthusiasm, motivating the church to take a second look at its mission and at itself. The youth can have a powerful influence, not only with their peers, but also with the rest of society. Their influence can outweigh that of the pastor and even of youth leaders when it comes to sharing their faith with other youth. I believe that the message of a crucified, risen, and soon-coming Savior would be carried to the world much more quickly if this potential army were trained and let loose.

Ellen White has some powerful things to say about the youth of the church and how effective they can be: "The church is languishing for the help of young men [and young women] who will bear a courageous testimony, who will with their ardent zeal stir up the sluggish energies of God's people, and so increase the power of the church in the world."[1] "Preachers, or laymen advanced in years, cannot have one half the influence upon the young that the youth, devoted to God, can have upon their associates. . . . With such an army of workers as our youth, rightly trained, might furnish, how soon the message of a crucified, risen, and soon-coming Saviour might be carried to the whole world."[2]

I had been the youth pastor for over 400 teens in a large church just outside London when I was invited to be senior pastor of a church in a rural town, with the added responsibility of being the district youth coordinator. Having a keen interest in youth ministry, I was anxious to meet with the youth of the church. The first week I preached, I noticed only a handful of young people in the congregation and asked the senior elder where all the kids were. I was informed that they were all present—all six of them. I calculated that there should have been around 40, given the number of families in the church, and so I questioned him again. After some pressing, he gave me a few names of some who had left the church. After talking with the church clerk, the leaders in the children's and youth divisions, and at length with the youth who remained, I had a list of over 40 names of young people who had once attended the church.

When I was asked to run a youth evangelistic campaign in a large city church, I asked the youth leadership team to give me a list of the names of youth who had left the church. It was my intention to start by visiting them. The leaders told me that they didn't lose many of their youth, but to humor me they would meet my request—the task of building a list would be easy. They started talking and in a few minutes had a handful of names for me. My experience told me that they should have a group totaling about one third of the number currently attending the church, hence, there should be over 100 names. After two meetings with the youth committee, we had a list of 135 young people who had once attended the church. This really shocked the youth team. They had only just begun. The number grew dramatically as they followed the steps outlined later in this book. This meant that 40 percent of the youth had left over a five-year period. "Out of sight, out of mind!" The statement is glib but true.

It is tragic that the church, challenged by the great commission of Christ (Matt. 28:18-20), has not realized the potential for evangelism that lies within its own young people. But what is even more tragic is that we spend millions of dollars on evangelism, often forgetting that our own youth need to be *saved*.

How big is the problem? How many youth leave the church each year and what is the most likely age that this happens? It is absolutely vital for each congregation to ask themselves these questions and take the time to seriously seek honest answers.

It is difficult to determine precisely how many youth leave the church annually. Most congregations are hesitant to remove names from their rolls, often keeping young people's names current long after they have left. Also, our church organization does not add names of youth to the church rolls until they have made the public commitment of baptism, so any figures collected based on church rolls will not reflect those who have left the church without ever being baptized. The number in this category is increased by the growing trend of young people leaving the decision for baptism until their late teens.

One of the first serious attempts to discover how many youth are inactive was undertaken by Roger Dudley at the Institute of Church Ministry at Andrews University. As part of a 10-year longitudinal study, Dudley obtained the names and addresses of 1,523 baptized young people ages 15 and 16. Approximately half of the subjects attended church academies, while the other half attended public schools. All of them were baptized and had made it clear that they intended to remain in the church in their adult years.

At the end of the study, when the subjects were 25 and 26 years old, approximately half did not respond to the final survey. One would be safe in assuming that of these, at least 50 percent had become inactive. Of those who did respond, 80 percent still claimed to be Adventists; however, of these, only 55 percent reported that they attended church regularly, while only 34 percent said they still attended Sabbath school. A conservative estimate is that 55 percent are leaving the church in each generation.[3] Even though these are the best statistics we have, they are still quite nebulous.

One of the surest indicators of whether young people will leave the church rests in their intention for future involvement. Do they plan to be involved in the church when they become adults? A major study of over 13,000 young people in the United States and Australia posed this question, and the results indicated that 28 percent were not planning to be in the church when they turned 40.[4] This means that nearly one third of our young people consciously plan to leave the church sometime in their adult years. Unfortunately, they often make this a reality before their teen years are over.

My personal experience as a church pastor and youth director supports the above findings and has revealed that the percentage of youth leaving the church on an ongoing basis ranges between 35 and 65 percent.

At what age are our youth most likely to leave the church? There is precious little research to help us with this question, and the answer varies from culture to culture and from country to country. After working with youth on three continents I believe it is fair to say that the critical period is at the end of high school, as they either enter the work force or begin tertiary study.[5] As youth assert their independence in this phase of life, one of the ways they do so is by questioning, reassessing, and often rejecting the values and beliefs of their parents and their church community.

The next question we need to tackle is why our young people choose to sever their connection with the church.

Over 1,200 young adults were surveyed in 1996 about the effectiveness of their church, school, and family in transmitting beliefs and values. The following popular responses to some of the questions were developed into a scale relating to why youth leave the church.[6]

"Adult members are living phony lives."

What happens in the mind of a young person who is chided by a church leader for inappropriate behavior with his girlfriend, when he finds out the same leader is having an affair with the deacon's wife? Too often we are ready to instruct with words and not through lifestyle. Do we truly seek the purity and self-control in our own hearts that we feel responsible to impart to our children? Young people have an uncanny ability to see through phony lives.

"The church places too much emphasis on nonessentials."

Baby boomers, now leaders in the church, will readily recall the disproportionate amount of time churches and church schools spent on the length of boys' hair and shortness of girls' dresses. What is more important, church standards or the youth themselves?

Many young people see some church "standards" as almost irrelevant. They struggle with the dry formality of much of the liturgy—forms and approaches to worship that seem so far removed from their world. To them, the real issues are drug problems, broken relationships, fighting parents who may end up in divorce court, or not making the grade at school. These are the questions they want the church to address, and they wonder if it can.

"Attitudes of older members are critical and uncaring."

A major study of 1,800 teens[7] revealed that 36 percent of 17- and 18-year-olds felt that the adult leaders in their church did not care about them. Fifty percent felt that the pastor had no time for them. Most church leaders and pastors are greatly saddened at these perceptions and probably think that they apply only to some other church. Unfortunately, they exist in the majority of locales. While they may not reflect the truth, perception is reality for the perceiver. Collectively, these perceptions create the feeling that the church as a whole is cold and unfriendly, which North American Division of Seventh-day Adventist academy students cite as the most likely reason they would sever connection with the church.[8]

"Church leaders are preoccupied with organization and not concerned with people."

It is easy to put policy before people, for the sake of order. A young man was recently invited to be a deacon. He had never worn a tie to church and the first time he was asked to take up the offering, he was dressed in his regular church apparel. The elder stopped the proceedings, and from the platform informed the young man: "If you are going to take up the offering in this church, you will wear a tie!" Terribly embarrassed, he gave the plate to the deacon standing next to him, walked out the door, and never returned.

"Worship services are dull and meaningless."

The celebrated English preacher, Charles Spurgeon, is reported to have said, "If the congregation goes to sleep, the deacon should get a long stick and poke the preacher." A poll of youth after the church service on any given week would find that only one in three say they find the services of the church interesting. The pastor holds a great responsibility to be both relevant and interesting in his preaching. It is my contention that it is a sin of enormous magnitude to portray the King of the universe as boring. "There He is. In the Temple again. Causing trouble. Speaking very differently from other preachers. Speaking with authority about sorrow and death. Penetrating the dark corners of human existence. Shattering illusion. Make no mistake about it; this is a dangerous man." You can't call this man boring![19]

An international preacher only occasionally sat with his young son in church. His son, deaf in one ear, would sit next to his mother each week and struggle with the proceedings. On those rare occasions when the preacher was home on the weekend, he would sit on the other side, the boy's deaf side. Invariably, at some point in the sermon the boy would whisper rather loudly, "Dad, I'm bored." When his father would tell him to be quiet, his son would think that he had not been heard and would repeat it that much louder, right under the preacher's nose: "Dad, I'm *bored*!" His father wanted to fling his head around and scream into his good ear, "Be quiet, kid, so am I!"

In 2005 all the young people between 12 and 18 years of age in the North American Seventh-day Adventist school system took part in a major survey called Valuegenesis. It sought to establish the effectiveness of the home, school, and church in transmitting values and beliefs to the youth, and in the results we get insight into the reasons they leave the church. For example,

20 percent cited dull and meaningless worship as one of the reasons they would walk away.[10]

"I do not want to be a hypocrite."

Driven by the desire to belong, many young people are baptized or formally become members at the early age of 11 or 12. Frequently, there is quite a lot of peer pressure for them to join the group. As they get older, some question why they did it and feel that they were not really committed at all. A young person's ability to see through the phony and hypocritical behavior of adults is surpassed only by their disgust of being perceived that way themself.

"The church is too restrictive."

Tony Campolo often describes Christian kids as those who "don't drink, don't smoke, don't chew, and don't go with girls who do!" Often, teens view the church's standards as arbitrary and out of touch, belonging to an age long since forgotten. A young person described his teen years like this:

> My mother taught me not to smoke—I don't.
> Or listen to a dirty joke—I don't.
> She told me that I must not think about intoxicating drink.
> At pretty girls I must not wink—I don't.
> Wild youth chase women, wine, and song—I don't.
> To stay out late is very wrong—I don't.
> I kiss no girls, not even one,
> I do not know how it is done,
> You would not think I have much fun—I don't![11]

It seems to teens that we have forgotten what it means to have fun—if we ever knew. Leaders tend to spend more time on the prohibitions and not enough on the freeing, liberating side of the good news. An inspired pen makes the following observation:

> Do not for a moment suppose that religion will make you sad and gloomy and will block up the way to success. The religion of Christ . . . in no way incapacitates you for the enjoyment of any real happiness. . . . It does not mantle the life in sackcloth; it is not expressed in deep-drawn

sighs and groans. No, no; those who in everything make God first, last, and best, are the happiest people in the world.[12]

When it comes to dealing with someone who has fallen, the church organization should follow the example of Jesus, as shown in His interaction with the woman caught in adultery. Instead, the church has appeared to favor a punitive approach. Too often, we forget that the root word of discipline is disciple. Discipline should not mean punishment, but the making of a better follower.

I recently led a number of workshops in which I taught listening skills to pastors and other church leaders. Given the opportunity to tell me their stories, two young pastors related similar accounts of the long-term pain they had suffered after being expelled from church schools. Their personal agony had kept them away from church for many years, and the pain lingered even after returning.

In another case students had been caught drinking and had even been captured on videotape holding up cans of beer for all to see. The school discipline committee was called, apparently only a formality, because students caught drinking had always been expelled, the last case being as recent as the end of the previous school year. Despite the new group's clear guilt, the school chaplain did some research and found that all of the young people expelled the previous year had left the church. He pleaded for the offenders to be kept in school. After a long, strenuous debate, all of the students finished the year and are still in the church nearly a decade later.

"I am attracted to a different lifestyle."

There is a basic honesty among the current generation of late teens and young adults. They admit that they find a different lifestyle much more attractive than what they see offered at church or at least what they have experienced in the Christian community. Adolescence is the stage for trying on new identities and seeing whether they can live in a different "house of belief." To them, there is a real appeal in the celebrity lifestyles that are presented on various TV shows.

"I have no real friends at church."

Another reason young people avoid church is a lack of friends. In a major review of youth values, Donald Poterski asserted that 90 percent of kids placed friendship at the top of the list of things they valued most.[13]

Friendship is the glue that binds youth to the church. Studies in church growth reveal that most people are introduced to the church by a friend and then remain members because of friendship.[14]

Andy Hickford notes that "peer pressure is the social and inner pressure to live up to the expectation of others in order to gain their acceptance and approval . . . taking huge amounts of teenagers' time and emotional energy."[15] When none of their friends go to church, there is added pressure to conform.

"The church does not allow me to think for myself."

This point of dissatisfaction will result from any organization that thinks it already has all the answers and does not allow room for questions. The North American and Australia/New Zealand Valuegenesis studies revealed that youth generally perceive the church as not encouraging them to think or question, and that the majority do not see the church as open to new ideas. The survey of North American students[16] revealed that only about half as many of the 18-year-olds as 12-year-olds find that the church challenges their thinking, encourages them to ask questions, is open to new ideas, and is warm and friendly. Even the 12-year-olds' perception of the church in these areas was not that high.

	North America		*Aust./NZ*	
	12	*18*	*12*	*18*
It challenges my thinking.	50% – 22%		79% – 62%	
It encourages me to ask questions.	46% – 23%		60% – 42%	
It is open to new ideas.	61% – 28%		51% – 39%	
It feels warm.	61% – 38%		79% – 61%	
It is friendly.	77% – 52%		77% – 62%	

The respondents cited the following issues as factors for their responses:
- Control—not allowed to think for themselves, problem with doctrines or with emphasis on nonessentials
- Lack of caring—felt that leaders or members didn't care about them
- Lack of meaning and purpose—felt that the church didn't offer real meaning for their lives
- Personal integrity—didn't want to appear hypocritical
- Discipline—problem with church or school discipline or restrictiveness, family issues

I would like to add three of my own reasons for youth leaving the church, drawn from my own interaction with them. These additions will sound familiar, and although the past 30 years have brought some minor changes, they bear the clear imprint of previous generations.[17]

Irrelevance

A growing number of youth, and even their parents, speak of the irrelevance of the church in their daily lives. Think about church services for a minute. Is it three hymns, a prayer, an offering, and a half-hour monologue every week? Or is it real adoration, worship, and celebration that is relevant to youth and other members of the congregation? North American youth highlighted irrelevant worship services as a reason they would leave, along with a cold and unfriendly church, no youth activities, and boring sermons.[18]

Unresponsiveness to Needs

When youth experience personal crises, they often feel that the church does nothing in response. Teen pregnancy is a growing phenomenon, despite most teenagers' strong mental assent that sex is only for marriage. For the church to take disciplinary action on a teenager in this situation is to further heighten the crisis. The young person is aware of the mistake—or even open sin—and does not need the church to compound the intense feelings of shame and regret. Many times, only the offending young woman is disciplined and the equally guilty young man is ignored, which opens the door wider for a disconnect with the church. If only the church were known for its support and not its censure. If only it could remember that it is a hospital for sinners and not a museum for saints.

We often miss what is really happening in the lives of troubled teens: "What we label the drug problem, the teen pregnancy problem, and the host of other problems of youth are merely the symptoms of a much larger, deep-rooted, and serious dilemma. Today's youth are at risk simply because they have no satisfactory reason to live."[19]

Family Issues

Still others cite their family as a reason why they do not want to belong to the church, a reason that is often ignored. A number of studies highlight the family as a key in understanding why young people stay or leave the church.[20] Brad Strahan has surveyed hundreds of college students in an attempt to see if there is a connection between the relationship a young person has with his parents and his images of God.[21] He is convinced that the quality of the parent-child bond is a more powerful predictor of a child's positive faith than the religiosity of the parent. A young person understands God's character much more clearly when they sees their parent demonstrating it every day.

The most effective parenting style for building the faith—as well as the psychological and emotional health—of a young person is one that shows affection and warmth and at the same time allows freedom and empowerment toward independence. Many young people see their Christian homes as restrictive and uncaring, a place where the parents' faith is valued more than the children themselves, let alone their independence. The temptation for parents to be overly protective—even if balanced with warmth and love—can make youth more dependent and less able to make decisions for themselves. Strahan is convinced that if the parents use religion to control, the young person will use religion to assert their independence.

Adolescence is a time of chaos and turmoil. Confused and fearful of the jumble of emotions inside, life can become very difficult for the young person and for all those around. Adding to the complexity is that late adolescence is the normal time to reconsider the value system of the family and the church. What an opportunity for the family, church congregation, and all those associated with these precious, storm-tossed youth to reach out with sincere interest, support, and love—just as Jesus would!

In the next chapter, we will examine how normal developmental issues impact the faith journey of our youth.

---

[1] Ellen G. White, *Messages to Young People* (Nashville: Southern Publishing Association, 1930), p. 25.

[2] *Ibid.*, pp. 204, 196.

[3] Actual numbers are given in Roger Dudley, *Why Our Teenagers Leave the Church* (Hagerstown: Review and Herald Publishing Association, 2000), pp. 27-37.

[4] V. B. Gillespie, M. J. Donahue, A. B. Gane, and E. Boyatt, *Valuegenesis Ten Years Later: A Study of Two Generations* (Riverside, Calif.: Hancock Center Publications, 2004), p. 288. The figure for Australia is 25 percent, but it is highest among the 17- and 18-year-olds.

[5] Sharon Parks, *The Critical Years: The Young Adult Search for a Faith to Live By* (San Francisco: Harper and Row, 1986), sees this period as crucial in the development of a faith that is owned and practiced.

[6] Although this survey was conducted in Australia and New Zealand, experience suggests that the reasons given appear to be similar throughout the western world. Although the ev-

idence in the United States is anecdotal, it does correlate with the Australia and New Zealand findings.

[7] A. Barry Gane, *Youth Ministry and the Transmission of Beliefs and Values* (Sydney: Avondale Academic Press, 1997).

[8] Gillespie, *op. cit.*

[9] Martin Bell.

[10] Gillespie, *op. cit.*

[11] Source unknown.

[12] White, *Messages to Young People*, p. 38.

[13] Donald Poterski, "A Mid-Decade Look at Youth Culture," *Youthworker* (Winter 1986), pp. 56-64.

[14] See chapter 3 ("Friendship Evangelism: Key to Reaching the Unchurched") in Monte Sahlin, *Sharing Our Faith With Friends Without Losing Either* (Hagerstown: Review and Herald Publishing Association, 1990).

[15] Andy Hickford, *Essential Youth: Why Your Church Needs Young People* (Eastbourne: Kingsway Publishing, 1998), p. 56.

[16] The table listed is taken from Roger L. Dudley, "Cause for Celebration or Concern? Insights From the Valuegenesis Study," *Journal of Adventist Youth Ministry* (Spring 1992), p. 29.

[17] In 1973, after studying the topic, Ila Zbaraschuk estimated that 50 percent of Adventist adolescents sever their connection with the church. She reported the following reasons most often given:

1. Church membership without personal conversion
2. Impersonal, uncaring attitude of older members
3. Phony-appearing lives of adult members
4. No sense of relevance to needs
5. Religion didn't make a difference in own life and didn't want to be a hypocrite
6. Absence of thinking for oneself
7. Misplaced emphasis, with nonessentials being too important
8. Church school disciplinary methods
9. Church leaders' preoccupation with organization
10. Poor quality of sermons

[18] Valuegenesis II data.

[19] Fran Sciacca, *Generation at Risk: What Legacy Are the Baby Boomers Leaving Their Kids?* (Chicago: Moody Press, 1990), p. 27.

[20] Mark DeVries, *Family-based Youth Ministry* (Downers Grove, Ill.: Intervarsity Press, 1994). This book spells out an approach to youth ministry that sells the family as a major contributory factor in successful youth work.

[21] Bradley J. Strahan, *Parents, Adolescents, and Religion* (Cooranbong, Australia: Avondale Academic Press, 1994).

Chapter 3

The Withdrawal Track

Our youths love luxury. They have bad manners, contempt for authority; they show disrespect for their elders and love to chatter in place of exercise. Children are now tyrants, not the servants of their households. They no longer rise when their elders enter the room. They contradict their parents, chatter before company, gobble up their food, and tyrannize their teachers." The author of this quote? Socrates, 400 B.C. Almost every generation has been critical of the next. It's easy to dismiss them, thinking they have little or nothing of value to offer.

Richard had not been to church for over a year when Ann approached the new pastor with the request, "Do you mind coming to see a friend of mine? He hasn't been to church for a while but I think you can help." The new pastor agreed, but arriving at the young man's home, he thought he may have made a mistake, as Richard let out a string of expletives and in no uncertain terms told him to leave. Ann refused to give up on her friend and pleaded with the pastor a second time, "Richard loves sports and is wanting to learn squash [a game similar to racquetball]. I heard you're pretty good, pastor—you could teach him."

Rich made it clear that the pastor couldn't teach him anything. Nevertheless, he agreed to play, telling the pastor he was going to give him a real thrashing. The outcome was quite the reverse and Richard was soundly beaten by his young, athletic opponent. The pastor again offered to teach him, and they agreed to meet every Monday morning for an hour. A friendship developed, and soon the pastor invited Rich to head up the games program at a youth retreat.

The church board erupted, "Pastor, you can't use him! He'll corrupt the other kids!"

"Please trust me on this," the pastor pleaded. "It could be a way for him to come back." Rich came and did his job well, but at worship time he sat as far away as he could, with his back to the pastor. However, by the end of the weekend, he was contributing to the discussion and even seemed to be enjoying it.

The reasons youth give for leaving the church are varied and every case has its own unique details. However, there are a number of common factors that form a predictable track. Figure 1 outlines the pathway walked by so many—away from the church.

Figure 1

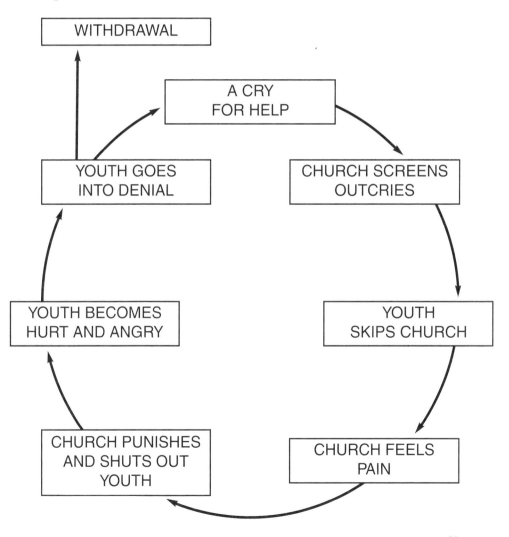

When a young person starts down this pathway, he is simply placing his feet in the footprints of countless youth before him. Recognizing these predictors helps youth workers to deflect youth from this perilous path and to redirect them back toward church.

The starting point is *a cry for help*. This can be as simple as, "I wish we had a basketball court like the boys club down the road has." Something as innocuous as this can release a tirade from an older member: "What are you thinking? Don't you know they don't have the truth? You can't be serious about wanting to go down there!" All the kid was asking for was some sort of social activity at his church. But this reaction may push him to go and find out that the boys club not only has a court, but a few caring youth workers, as well. And because of the relationships he finds there, he may begin to feel that there is not much point in going to his own church anymore.

Many times the cry for help will be accompanied by tears. A youth speaker found himself being shadowed by a pretty young woman. It seemed that he bumped into her every time he turned around. It was clear that she wanted his attention—that she needed to talk to someone. After an hour of meaningless chatter, the speaker headed off to another appointment. More talks followed, and every time tears trembled just below the surface, but she could not bring herself to share her pain. They sat down again to talk at a youth convention. She had brought her sister with her this time, and as soon as everyone was seated, she blurted out, "My grandfather . . ." Her sentence was cut off by her sister, who began to cry, "Oh, no! He did it to me, too." The youth speaker didn't understand. What had happened? Amid the tears of these young women, the story finally tumbled out. Their grandfather, a church elder, had sexually abused each of his granddaughters. They had suffered alone, too ashamed to share with each other—until their cry for help was finally heard.

The young woman had gone to her pastor for help. He responded by telling her not to be silly, that because her grandfather was a leader in the church, he would never do that. He warned her to stop making up stories, and each word of rebuke compounded her pain. She felt *screened out*, rejected by the very people she had sought for help. It was a very short distance to the next step, to altogether avoid the meeting place of those who screened out her cries—to *skip church*.

Many church members find it difficult to believe that sexual abuse could be present in the church. According to Valuegenesis data collected in both North America and Australia, almost one third of young women in the church, and one in ten young men in the church, have reported being sexually abused (see Figure 2). These numbers do not change with socioeconomic, racial, or religious status, and they parallel reports of abuse in the community. There is some evidence that the figures are higher for rigidly enmeshed religiously fundamental groups. Sadly, the perpetrators are usually acquaintances, and many are church members, with nearly 20 percent holding leadership positions (Figures 3 and 4). One can only imagine the severe damage sexual abuse can have on a young person and on her relationship to the church, which was designed to be part of the network ensuring her safety.

Figure 2

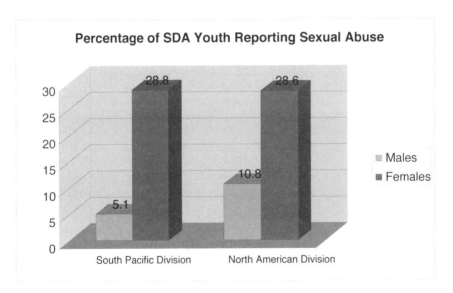

Figure 3

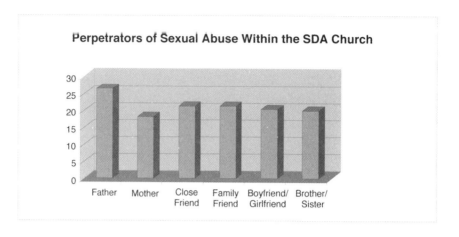

Figure 4

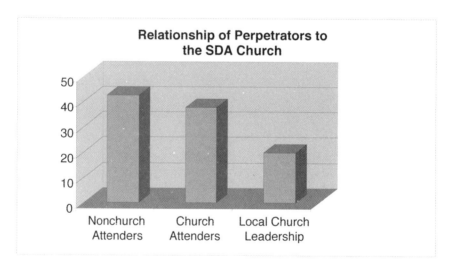

It seems almost incomprehensible that *the church corporately feels pain*. But many within the church feel hurt and rejected when a young person chooses to remove themself from the body of believers. Often, those who feel hurt have no knowledge of why the young person has stopped coming and see no other option but to chalk it up to yet another wild youth choosing to do their own thing.

When a young person stops coming to church, they find other things to do during church time. On their way to church Sabbath morning, other church members may see the youth involved in sports or hanging around the "wrong part of town." Assumptions are made, reports are given. Those young people still attending church are warned by their parents and youth leaders to stay clear of this bad influence. Barriers are raised that tend to compound the problems of the young person, who now feels *punished* and *shut out*. Richard had been warned not to hang around the good kids at church. Fortunately, Ann would not let go of their friendship that easily.

The teen years are times of hormonal surges, and sometimes kids are tempted to experiment with their sexuality. Despite its strong stand against premarital sex, the church is not immune from teen pregnancy. When Christian kids fall to temptation, their predicament is often worse than that of other kids because their moral position precludes the use of birth control. "We did not plan to make love." Pregnant teens will cry out for help, and when they do, they are often told that they brought this on themselves and that they have to bear the consequences. At the very time they need support, they are often rejected and disciplined. Many churches will disfellowship teens to make an example of them, to frighten others from following the same path.

A mother came to a pastor with the question, "What are you going to do about Christine?" Christine was pregnant—it was obvious to everyone. She had talked to the pastor and he knew who the father was. His response was quick: "What are *you* doing about Christine; are you knitting some baby clothes?"

"No, pastor. You have to call the church board and have her disciplined!"

"I will call the church board and discipline the father of the expected twins." After he revealed that the father of Christine's babies was this woman's son, the wind quickly left her sails. Discipline was administered and it helped Christine become a better disciple. Interwoven with the discipline was the clear message that she was part of a church family who cared for her and would support her through this time of crisis. Discipline without this message drives young people away feeling hurt and resentful and slams the door on the possibility of the church ministering to them in the future.

Soon the hurt and resentment turns to *anger*. The rejected young person may begin pointing out the sins of other people in the congregation, spreading seeds of tension that grow into bitter weeds extremely difficult to remove. I have met countless people who return to church in midlife still struggling to shed the hurt and resentment they experienced as teenagers.

It does not take long before resentment turns to *denial*. "I don't care— I never really liked going to church anyway. I don't need those people. I'm happy to be away from that bunch of clowns and hypocrites." At this stage the young person is not far from severing connection permanently. They may even send a letter to let the church know that they do not want any further contact.

The church often interprets this final move as irreparable. Apostasy has taken place. There is no hope. Or is there? John Savage, a researcher and pastor, has found that if young people are visited within the first two months of being absent, around 80 percent will return. Immediate action is vital, as the percentage drops the longer the person has been missing.

Anxiety is the hidden root of many teen behaviors mistakenly labeled as rebellion. Savage has shown that most disconnections from the church can be traced back to an anxiety-provoking event. He says that these usually come in clusters and that the church is often the source of the young person's feeling of disequilibrium through a perceived snub, lack of care, or censure.*

What takes place in the teen years is expected and is part of the human journey. The struggle to achieve identity, understand gender roles, and establish owned faith are all part of the process. Church leaders, especially youth workers, absolutely must understand this process and provide youth with the loving advocacy necessary to keep unchecked anxiety from leading them to permanent separation from the church.

In the next chapter we will look at some of the developmental challenges that confront young people on the journey toward maturity.

------

*John S. Savage, "Ministry to Missing Members," *Leadership* spring quarter 1987), pp. 116-121.

Chapter 4

Growing Up?

Many a parent of teenagers has exclaimed in total exasperation, "I don't know what makes kids today act the way they do; you often think you are trying to communicate with a different life form. I just don't understand them. What makes them tick?" Psychology has helped us understand the long and often tortuous journey from childhood into independent adulthood. Studies in sociology give us an insight into the fact that like their parent's generation, they too are a product of their society, their education, their family, and their environment as a whole. We will deal with these generational differences in a later chapter.

Patricia Hersch observed teens for years before launching her landmark study, *A Tribe Apart*. She aptly states:

> Adolescence is a journey, a search for self in every dimension of being. It is about dreams, fears, and hopes, as much as about hormones, SAT scores, and fashion. It is about endless possibilities as well as dead ends. It is searching, testing, experimentation. It is growth: it is undeniable that the young person at any point in time will be different one year later—different physically, intellectually, emotionally, and experientially.[1]

Is it any wonder they are sometimes difficult to understand?

Identity Formation

Noted psychologist Erik Erikson stated the theory that all people navigate their way through a series of crises as they journey through life. He contends that the crisis in the middle to late teen years is that of developing a personal identity. This involves trying on a series of identities that are often very different from the one in use up until that time. This is often frightening for parents, teachers, and church leaders who do not know how to relate to this new person living with them or sitting in their class-room or church.[2]

James Marcia expanded on Erikson's identity crisis theory when he de-vised an identity status pattern consisting of four specific "places" where teens tend to settle, if only for a while, on the journey to discover their iden-tity.[3] These four places are:

Identity Diffusion

A young person at this place has not begun to develop a sense of identity. They tend to be confused and withdrawn and suffer from feelings of dis-comfort and not belonging.[4]

Identity Foreclosure

A teen in this place has merely accepted the identity given to them and has not yet struggled to achieve their own. It can appear that they have achieved their own identity, as they often behave well and submit to author-ity. However, be warned that as they leave home, a new, very different person often emerges.

Identity Moratorium

At this place the teen recognizes that they are "weighing up" and are in the midst of trying on various identities. Their struggle is marked by inde-cision and insecurity, and their behavior lets those around them know that they need space to maneuver.

Identity Achieved

Ah, the goal is reached. Having wrestled with alternatives, they have ar-rived at a personal commitment to an integrated identity. They know who they are and are comfortable with the knowledge.

Healthy families and wise church leaders desire that adolescents nego-tiate this period of their lives successfully, achieving their own identity and owning a clear set of values. They would rather see them governed by inter-nalized values than controlled by parents, church, or school.

It is clear that by the time a child has reached the middle teens, they are in the midst of sorting out their own identity. This can be a time of uncertainty and crisis.[5] This process of self-discovery and construction of a personal value system often requires separation from parents and a questioning of the values that the family has sought to transfer. The young person, either consciously or unconsciously, senses the need to remove themself from the house of their childhood in order to build their own "house of belief" in which they can comfortably live. To parents who understandably misinterpret this tumultuous process as senseless rebellion and/or a personal rejection, it is reassuring to know that teenagers do not suddenly cease to be what they once were. Adolescence builds on the experiences of childhood; it does not erase them.[6] The developing adult ultimately holds on to, or owns, much of the parents' value system that they are now questioning.

Teenagers live in the shadow of the ever-present question, "Who am I?" This question is answered, not by the young person, but by others. Adler and Towne make this statement: "The evaluations others make of us are the mirror by which we know ourselves; and since children are trusting souls who have no other way of viewing themselves, they accept at face value both the positive and negative evaluations of the apparently all-knowing and all-powerful adults around them."[7]

This is why young people are so concerned about being accepted and are so conscious of the statements of others, especially those of their peers. The power of peer endorsements often gives peers a greater pulling power than the family. Their drive for acceptance dictates their behavior and explains why they do what they do. Donald Ratcliff and James Davies state:

> The general function of the youth subculture is to compensate for the failure of the main culture to provide a definite status, a feeling of acceptance, and need-satisfactions unique to the adolescents. Such collective stirrings of modern youths are largely a consequence of the adolescent crisis in postindustrial society. The formation of a teenage subculture compensates for this crisis. It provides temporary security and a collective bonding mechanism.[8]

Stages of Development

James W. Fowler, director of the Center for Faith Development at Emory University, recognized the possibility of specifically defined stages in the area of faith, building on the theories of Erik Erikson in the area of psychosocial development, Piaget in cognitive development, and Laurence Kolberg in moral development.

Once a person has successfully negotiated the challenge of a particular stage, they come to a position of equilibrium and may remain there for some time, until they are challenged by the issues of the next stage. An adolescent who has achieved identity and has moved on in search of intimacy and fulfillment retains a knowledge and understanding of the issues that they have worked through; however, their insights into the stage ahead are limited, and in some cases, nonexistent.

According to Piaget, it is not until the final stage he calls *formal operations*, which comes in the adolescent years, that a person has the cognitive, or reasoning, ability to work through the issues of identity. Around the time of puberty, a child begins to think abstractly, theorize, idealize, and dream about what might be. They have reached the stage when they are capable of adult-style reasoning, even though their vocabulary and experience may not allow for the full understanding or expression of their thoughts. Lawrence O. Richards explains why Piaget's work has important implications for the transmission of values, or Christian education. He introduces three important concepts that help us understand adolescent cognitive development:

1. Cognitive growth progresses through invariable stages that are analogous to physical growth.
2. Learning involves a transaction between the person and their environment. They construct a reality picture to explain the world and their place in it.
3. A person's environment combines with internal developmental changes to produce an equilibrium that periodically restructures their view of reality. It is striking to realize just how much cognitive development takes place, not in childhood years, but in the teens and twenties.[9]

Laurence Kohlberg, building on the work of Piaget, identified a series of approaches to moral thinking, or reasoning, a number of which are confirmed by Valuegenesis study results. During Kohlberg's third stage, the young person's moral reasoning is colored by their need for approval. At this stage, they become aware of other people's views of them in personal terms: "I see you seeing me; I construct the me I think you see."[10] The young person behaves in a way that gains approval from authority figures—the "right" way—because they know that this pleases.

In Kohlberg's fourth stage, the young person looks at the world in terms of law and order. It makes sense to them that things should be done according to law, so that order might be maintained. They reason that law is for the good of the majority of people. It is by authority and fixed rules that they determine the rightness or wrongness of any action, and they view things as black or white, leaving no room for gray areas.

Some young people 18 and older may enter the fifth stage of Kohlberg's scheme.[11] Fowler summarizes this stage as follows: "Stage five recognizes the relativity of most social rules and laws but affirms the importance of upholding them in the interest of impartiality and because they are the social contract. Some values and rights, however, are not relative and must be upheld in any society and regardless of majority opinion. These include life, liberty, and freedom from arbitrary personal or class oppression. [12] Although the Valuegenesis study does not view faith maturity in terms of Kohlberg's approach to moral thinking, a comparison of the two sheds light on common issues, such as young people's levels of social consciousness and attitudes toward people of different races and socioeconomic groupings.

Stages of Faith

Erik Erikson speaks of faith, or belief structure, in terms of ideology and suggests that it becomes "the guardian of identity." He asserts that a belief system is the guide that helps the developing adolescent shape their life, and that without some ideological commitment, however implicit, they will suffer confusion of values. Erikson states: "If the earliest stage bequeathed to the identity crisis [is] an important need for trust in oneself and in others, then clearly the adolescent looks most fervently for men and ideas to have faith in, which also means men and ideas in whose service it would seem worthwhile to prove oneself trustworthy."[13]

It was James Fowler who gave credibility to the concept of developmental stages in faith growth, although he speaks of faith in terms of making sense out of life, and getting meaning out of it, rather than as trusting in a supernatural being. He identified a six-stage process, with each stage building on the last. However, he does not contend that every person progresses through all the stages and ends up at stage six, stating that there are many who do not progress beyond the faith stage of their childhood. I believe there is room to roughly align Fowler's faith stages with age, and it appears that his stages three and four clearly coincide with the adolescent years.

Fowler has given titles to his stages, which in and of themselves have little or no meaning to the layman. Stage three, the "synthetic-conventional," is when the person's insight and experience grows beyond theirself and their immediate surroundings to the larger world. During this stage, their faith is central in helping them relate to and interpret a more complex spectrum of people and ideas, providing a basis for identity and outlook.

Fowler tells us that faith during the adolescent period is still basically "unowned," as adolescents continue to merely adopt the views of God and the world from significant others. He asserts: "Values, commitments, and relationships are seen as central to identity and worth, at a time when worth is heavily keyed to the approval and affirmation of significant others."[14] The individual does not yet have a secure hold on their identity, or confidence in their personal judgment, to the extent that they can construct and maintain an independent view. Fowler sees this sort of activity taking place in stage four, which he calls the "individuating-reflexive."

In Fowler's view it is not until toward the end of adolescence that a young person begins to seriously look at concepts of the world and to consider a commitment to a lifestyle and belief system deeply rooted enough to affect their attitudes and behaviors. The strength that begins to emerge toward the end of adolescence involves a capacity for reflecting on their own identity, where they stand in the scheme of things, where they are heading, and their worldview in relation to others and to God. It is at this time that they begin to individuate,[15] forming perspectives that are truly internalized and owned.

There are a number of books written on faith development, but the reader is advised to look seriously at James Fowler's *Stages of Faith*,[16] Bruce Powers' *Growing Faith*,[17] and for the late adolescent, the concepts developed by Sharon Parks in *The Critical Years*.[18]

John Westerhoff III[19] is another pioneer addressing the concept of faith development in young people. In his much simpler approach, the young person progresses from an experienced faith to an owned faith. At the first level, the child experiences the "faith of significant others." Westerhoff asserts that experience is foundational to faith; therefore, the experiences of trust, love, and acceptance are the factors that foster and grow faith.

Westerhoff's second level, which overlaps with our study of adolescents, he identifies as "affiliate faith." If the child experiences faith in a way that meets their needs, then they may progress to the place where they wish to belong to the community that has accepted them. This desire to affiliate, or belong, is often seen around the ages of 10 to 12, which is the most common time for baptisms to occur.

Westerhoff's third level is "searching faith." This is the time when many parents become extremely concerned as the young person, who so obviously accepted and endorsed the family's belief system in their younger years, is now beginning to question it. They begin to experiment with alternate views, trying on different approaches in order to make sense out of life.

The last level is "owned faith." The young person arrives here when they have chosen and internalized a value system for themself. Their searching has not completely ended, because meaning-making continues to demand searching and reassessment, but they have incorporated a faith that they are willing to stand by. It is no longer a faith that they experienced through a significant other, such as a parent, or is the result of the drive to affiliate with a group within their immediate community. Their actions, attitudes, and behaviors are now motivated from within and the locus of control is internal. It is here that they testify to a personal knowledge of God, to their acceptance of God's action in Jesus, and to their desire to conduct their life in accordance with God's will through personal commitment.[20]

Looking at faith in the terms that we've outlined above means a change of emphasis. Faith is now seen as the process of making meaning out of life through the evaluation of alternatives. This view does not ignore the spiritual content of a specific faith, but describes its integration into the life of the young person. A growing body of evidence suggests that when a young person internalizes their religious belief, they are less prone to depression and anxiety than those who are coerced, controlled, or motivated by an external authority in the area of religious belief and practice.[21]

Table 1 indicates how the different theories interact and overlap. The shaded area is where the majority of young people are when they sever connection with their church.

Table 1
STAGES OF DEVELOPMENT

AGE	SOCIO-EMOTIONAL (Erikson)	COGNITIVE (Piaget)	MORAL (Kohlberg)	FAITH (Fowler/Westerhoff)	
0 – 1	Trust vs. Mistrust	Sensorimotor			
2 – 3	Autonomy vs. Shame/Doubt	Preoperational (Preconceptual)	Punishment and Obedience Orientation		Experienced Faith
4 – 6	Initiative vs. Guilt	(Intuitive)		Intuitive–Projective	
7 – 11	Industry vs. Inferiority	Concrete Operations	Instrumental Relativist Orientation	Mythic–Literal	Affiliate Faith
12 – 17	Identity vs. Role Confusion	Formal Operations	Interpersonal Concordance Orientation (Good boy/Nice girl) Law and Order Orientation	Synthetic–Conventional	Searching Faith
18 – 29	Intimacy vs. Isolation		Social Contract Legalistic Orientation	Individuating–Reflexive Conjunctive	Owned Faith
30 – 50	Generativity vs. Stagnation		Universal Ethical Principles Orientation	Universalizing	
51 +	Ego Integrity vs. Despair				

Recent studies in the area of neuroscience have revealed that the teenage brain undergoes a dramatic growth spurt. [22] It was previously thought that this took place only in the early childhood years, but through MRI scans, we now know that it takes place again during the teen years. The teen brain is like the adult brain in many ways, but differs in some significant areas, at least partially explaining why normally sensible teens sometimes make inexplicable decisions.

Shannon Brownlee interviewed a number of leading scientists in the area and, speaking of the teenager, reports:

Different regions of his brain are developing on different timetables. For instance, one of the last parts to mature is in charge of making sound judgments and calming unruly emotions. And the emotional centers in the teenage brain have already been revving up, probably under the influence of sex hormones. This imbalance may explain why your intelligent 16-year-old doesn't think twice about getting into a car driven by a friend who is drunk, or why your formerly equable 13-year-old can be hugging you one minute and then flying off the handle the next.[23]

Brownlee goes on to cite Jay Giedd, expert child psychiatrist at the National Institute of Mental Health in Bethesda, Maryland: "Adolescence is a time of tumultuous change in the brain. Teenagers are choosing what their brains are going to be good at—learning right from wrong, responsibility or impulsiveness, thinking or video games."

It appears that the reason teens can have real trouble making consistently sound judgments is that the prefrontal cortex, the part of the brain responsible for control, is still developing, making them more likely to be driven by emotional response rather than by reason. This may explain why they will mentally assent to abstinence from a certain "at-risk" behavior, such as drinking alcohol, but will simultaneously take a drink when a friend offers it to them at a party.

Adolescence is the season of life when people are most likely to experiment, not only with identity, but also with behavior.[24] Whether an experiment becomes a lifestyle or not will largely depend on the strength of the bond the adolescent has with parents, church, and the type of friends with whom they choose to associate.[25] Duffy Robbins, longtime youth ministry educator, highlights the importance of the bond between youth and significant older people when he states: "One of the recurring themes of developmental research is the impact of relationships on virtually every area of development."[26]

Unfortunately, we find that parents do not spend the time necessary to develop and maintain that bond, as David Breskin points out:

First off, chances are an adolescent's parents are divorced. Suicides come disproportionately from broken homes, and the increase in young suicides parallels the giddy divorce rate, now over 50 percent, and the highest in the world. Married or divorced, the adolescent's mother works outside the home. She prides herself on how quickly she goes back to work after he/she is born. (That the father is absent or away at work is a given.) His/her parents subcontract responsibility for raising him/her to day-care surrogates, nurses and sitters, and to Johnny himself. . . . There's no extended family around for him, not with the geographic mobility for which Americans are famous. The moving is hard on him. He must keep readapting to new environments.

American parents spend less time with Johnny than any other parents in the world. While he's a teenager, they spend an average of 14 minutes a week communicating with him. By the time Johnny graduates from high school, he'll have spent more time with his blue, flickering electronic parent than doing anything else but sleeping; he'll have seen 20,000 hours of TV, 350,000 commercials, about 18,000 killings. The family doesn't talk—they watch. On TV problems resolve themselves in 30-minute spans. It's his only problem-solving role model, and it's unrealistic.

That his life is not as exciting as the life on TV may come as a disappointment. His pain comes as a nasty shock, and he'll learn to escape rather than cope. He has far more access to booze, dope, pills, coke, than any previous generation of kids, and at an earlier age. He also has easy access to the genitals of the opposite sex, and the sooner he scores, the more difficulty he'll have with intimacy later on. Chances are increasing that he will be sexually or physically abused by an adult at an early age.

Competition is tremendous. If he is middle or upper-middle class, his parents have already told him he had better start running, and fast, because the pie is shrinking. The number of his peers has doubled in 20 years, but the opportunities haven't. There are only so many spots on the basketball team or in the law firm. He feels pressure to be perfect. This "cohort effect" means he lives in a downwardly mobile, increasingly Darwinian world. It's called, trendily, the end of childhood. Johnny quickly learns that good grades and other tangible achievements are the currency in which he trades for his parents' approval and concomitant permissiveness. The parents see the equation differently: They provide material well-being; he delivers good grades in return. His parents are permissive because it's easier to say yes than no. Besides, they don't know what rules are valid anymore. Everything in this world is negotiable now: Everything is shades of gray, and all that matters is green.

They treat the kid like a little adult because they want him to be a little adult. They seek his friendship and fear his disapproval. When they give him too much freedom, he secretly desires rules; but they don't want to tell him about sex, about values, pain, problem solving, living with limitations. All is uncertain, nothing is shocking, everything is tolerated.

All told, Johnny lives in a bizarre warp of freedom and pressure at a stage of his life when neither is appropriate: when pressure makes him brittle and freedom's just another word for everything to lose.[27]

---

[1] Patricia Hersch, *A Tribe Apart* (New York: Fawcett Columbine, 1998), p. 17.

[2] The vast majority of teens end up adopting the value system of their parents.

[3] James Marcia, "Identity in Adolescence," in Joseph Adelson, ed., *Handbook of Adolescent Psychology* (New York: John Wiley and Sons, 1980), pp. 159-181.

[4] The second report on the Valuegenesis project, Bradley J. Strahan, *Parents, Adolescence and Religion*, gives far more detail on the process outlined by Marcia.

[5] Some scholars question that adolescence necessarily means turbulence and actually contend that anxieties traditionally believed to be part of adolescence relate to only the "deviant 10 percent of the adolescent population." (See Albert Bandura, "The Stormy Decade: Fact or Fiction?" *Psychology in the School* 1 (1964): 224, cited in Zuck, Roy B., ed., Warren S. Benson, "Adolescents, An Age of Acceleration and Crisis," in *Youth Education in the Church* (Chicago: Moody Press, 1987), p. 15. It is true that there are a number of youth who appear to pass through adolescence without much apparent psychological trauma, but it has been my experience that these are in the minority.

[6] Francis Bridger, *Children Finding Faith* (London: Scripture Union, 1988), p. 64.

[7] Ronald B. Adler and Neil Towne, *Looking Out Looking In: Interpersonal Communication* (Sydney: Holt, Rinehart, and Winston, 1987), p. 36.

[8] Donald Ratcliff and James Davies, eds., *Handbook of Youth Ministry* (Birmingham: Religious Education Press, 1991), p. 9, cited by Marlene LeFever, "Learning," *Youthworker* (Fall 1991), p. 31. The Balswicks have this to say about peer influence and the creation of a youth subculture: "The creation of an adolescent subculture is an attempt to establish identity. One

learns from peer groups to wear the right clothes, effect the right hairstyle, play the 'in' music, speak the 'in' language. The greater the adolescent's insecurity, the greater the slavish obedience to doing all the right things as sanctioned by the peer group." Balswick, Jack O. and Judith K., *The Family: A Christian Perspective on the Contemporary Home,* (Grand Rapids: Baker, 1989), p. 137.

[9] Lawrence O. Richards, "Cognitive Development of Adolescents," in Zuck, Roy B., and Warren S. Benson, *Youth Education in the Church* (Chicago: Moody Press, 1987), p. 109.

[10] James Fowler, *Stages of Faith* (New York: Harper and Row, 1981), p. 72.

[11] Some see a halfway stage between four and five, in which the young person takes a cynical ethical relativism motivated by principle. This is a period of real questioning concerning the rights of the individual. See Sharon Parks, *The Critical Years: Young Adults and the Search for Meaning, Faith, and Commitment* (San Francisco: Harper, 1986).

[12] Fowler, p. 83.

[13] Erik H. Erikson, *Identity: Youth and Crisis* (New York: W. W. Norton, 1968), pp. 128, 129.

[14] Craig Dykstra and Sharon Parks, eds., *Faith Development and Fowler* (Birmingham, Ala.: Religious Education Press, 1986), p. 29.

[15] To individuate means to become one's own person. See James E. Loder, *The Logic of the Spirit: Human Development in Theological Perspective* (San Francisco: Jossey-Bass, 1998), p. 286.

[16] Fowler, *Stages of Faith.*

[17] Bruce P. Powers, *Growing Faith* (Nashville: Broadman Press, 1982).

[18] Sharon Parks, *The Critical Years: The Young Adult Search for a Faith to Live By* (San Francisco: Harper and Row, 1986).

[19] John H. Westerhoff III, *Will Our Children Have Faith?* (East Malvern, Vic: Dove Communications Pty. Ltd., 1976).

[20] *Ibid.,* pp. 91-99.

[21] See R. M. Ryan, S. Rigby, and K. King, "Two Types of Religious Internalization and Their Relations to Religious Orientations and Mental Health," *Journal of Personality and Social Psychology* 65: 3, pp. 586-596.

[22] B. S. Begley, "Getting Inside the Teenage Brain," *Newsweek* (February 28, 2000); S. Durston, Pol Hulshoff, E. Hilleke, B. J. Casey, Jay N. Giedd, Jan K. Buitelaar, and Herman Van England, "Anatomical MRI of the Developing Human Brain: What Have We Learned?" *Journal of the American Academy of Child and Adolescent Psychiatry* 40, no. 9 (2001): pp. 1012-1020; S. Brownlee, "Inside the Teen Brain: Changes Inside May Explain Turmoil on the Outside," *US News and World Report: Mysteries of the Teen Years* (May 10, 2005): pp. 15-21.

[23] Shannon Brownlee, "Inside the Teen Brain: Changes Inside May Explain Turmoil on the Outside."

[24] Erik Erikson, *Identity, Youth, and Crisis* (New York: Norton, 1968).

[25] B. B. Benda and R. F. Corwyn, "A Test of a Model With Reciprocal Effects Between Religiosity and Various Forms of Delinquency Using 2-stage Least Squares Regression," *Journal of Social Service Research* (1997): pp. 22, 27-52.

[26] Duffy Robbins, *This Way to Youth Ministry: An Introduction to the Adventure* (Grand Rapids, Mich.: Zondervan Publishing House, 2004), pp. 242, 243.

[27] David Breskin, "Dear Mom and Dad," *Rolling Stone* (November, 1984).

Chapter 5

Marching to a Different Drum—Understanding a New Generation

Growing up, it seemed like I couldn't win with my grandma. As a child of the sixties, I fluctuated between wanting to look like a Beatle and Elvis Presley. Nanna would chide, "Get a haircut—you look like a girl." If I slicked it down with grease, her response was, "Why do you want to look like a hoodlum?" So I had it all shaved off, only to suffer the response, "What, now you want to look like a jailbird?"

Before our modern era, generation after generation of teenagers appeared to accept the value system, religion, and worldview of their parents with little alteration or rebellion. Today, it seems that the endless tussles between the generations are no longer limited to raised voices at home but have also entered the church. It seems that everything is up for argument, that nothing is going to be left alone. The style of the preacher, the leading of worship, the music that accompanies our praise, our approach to supporting the cause with offerings, and even our prayers, are being re-assessed as to their level of meaning. What some see as worship renewal is seen by others as being covered with the devil's fingerprints! Let's pull back the curtain and see what may be causing this passionate sparring.

We are constantly reminded that the generation who survived World War II not only made the nation great, but also built the church. We are told that they "had it right," that if it worked then, it should work now, and that if it's not working, we just aren't doing it right. Starting around 30 years ago, these preboomers largely controlled the church at every level, serving in every position from local church elder to conference president. Today, a strong and unexpected affinity appears to be blooming between them and teenagers in the church; they seem less critical of the kids than do their own parents.

Table 1 shows the different approaches the various generations take toward church. The older generation has an unquestioning loyalty to the church. Pastors faithfully minister out of calling and duty, and they never retire. For them, church is very formal, orderly, and program-oriented. Reverence is about silence, audience participation is limited, and hymns, accompanied by organ or piano, form the center of worship. Overall, this group most appreciates expository preaching, usually delivered in formal oratory style for a mainly auditory audience. The preacher tells you what he is going to tell you, then tells you, and finishes by telling you what he has told you. These preboomers, who ran the church for so long, are now well into retirement and are in the process of releasing control.

Baby boomers now fill church leadership roles, and as the "me generation" are now ensuring that their needs are finally being met. Their pastors minister for personal satisfaction, and their people-oriented congregations are highly relational. They applaud innovation and seek greater involvement in the running of the church. The sermons they appreciate are more informational and conversational. They are far more visual and appreciate a higher level of audience participation. Guests prefer to remain anonymous.

The baby busters (Generation X), now in their late twenties,[1] are the smallest of the generations and probably the most misunderstood. We have witnessed them leaving the church in droves, their complaint of institutional religion being utterly irrelevant ringing in our ears as they walk out the doors. As a product of their time, they are driven by issues. Their loyalty to causes is almost religious and they have powerfully raised concern about global warming and pollution. They crave spontaneity and variety in worship, while at the same time hungering for community. For this reason they see talking to each other as a vital part of church. They are comfortable with praise songs imported from other church traditions and use a wide variety of instruments to accompany worship. They are comfortable with a much more relaxed approach to leadership.

The current generation of youth and young adults has been called Generation Y, mosaics, and most often, millennials.[2] (See Table 2 for an in-depth overview of this generation.) They, as many generations of youth before them, are greatly influenced by their peers and there is a strong drive toward deeper relationships. They are closer to their parents than the busters were. Despite being fairly conservative, they also demand change in most areas of their lives. They want flexible working hours and are not fazed by the idea of having a number of jobs throughout their lifetime.

At church music deeply affects them, and they seek a wide variety. They relate best with sermons that are narrative in style. Since building community is important to them, they talk openly in church. Many millenials see themselves as spiritual but divorced from the organized church. Multiculturalism, globalism, and heroism have powerfully shaped their value system, and they abhor the idea of anyone being put down because of race, culture, or religion. They are used to the advocacy of their parents, which has made them confident, even optimistic, and they are happy to volunteer for service projects benefiting complete strangers. They will raise large amounts of money to participate in short-term mission projects. Millenials seek strong but flexible leadership that will challenge them, recognizing their need to work closely with their friends. Their dependence on technology is unrivaled by any other generation.

It is easy to see why there are difficulties in communication between the generational groups in the church. Each one is a product of its time and relates to issues passionately, often at the opposite end of the spectrum. While the needs of one generation are being met in worship, another generation may perceive the means of its fulfillment as irrelevant or even sacrilegious.

Postmodernism

For decades we had talked about a generation gap that made communication difficult. We are now dealing with a complete change in the way people process information and make sense of the world. This fundamental shift has affected all generations to some extent, but none more so than the millenials. Postmodernism represents the most profound mind-set leap in over 200 years. It has changed the way people view themselves, their community, truth, reality, and even the way they find meaning in life. Many social observers see it as a reaction against the long, dry reign of rationalism, in which answers to all questions could be found empirically and logically through the sheer power of reason.[3]

Sally Morgenthaler speaks of the impact of postmodernism:

Postmodernism asserts that there is more than one way of knowing. Besides pure reason, there is intuition and emotion, and truth itself goes

Table 1

GENERATIONAL DIFFERENCES WITHIN THE CHURCH

Pre-Boomers	Baby Boomers	Baby Busters	Millennials
Religious Factors			
Commitment to Christ = commitment to church	Commitment to Christ = commitment to relationships	Commitment to Christ = commitment to community	Commitment to Christ = commitment to peer group
Program-oriented	People-oriented	Community-oriented	Peer group-oriented
Money to missions	Money to people	Money to causes	Money to ministry in which they are involved
In-depth Bible study/prayer	Practical Bible study/prayer/sharing	Issue-oriented Bible study/prayer/sharing	Fundamentals-based Bible study
Loyalty to denomination	Loyalty to people	Loyalty to causes	Loyalty to peer group
Minister out of duty	Minister for personal satisfaction	Minister to confront issues	
Programs			
Relate to missions	Relate to people	Relate to causes	Relate to peers
Stress in-depth Bible study/prayer	Stress fellowship, support groups	Stress Bible studies on issues	Stress Bible studies on fundamentals
Maintain stability	Use variety	Use variety	Use variety
Focus on marriage, retirement	Focus on marriage, family	Focus on marriage, singles	Focus on relationships
Formal, orderly	Relational	Spontaneous	Open to change
Maintain status quo	Applaud innovation	Invite variety, change	Demand change
Encourage contact with baby busters	Encourage involvement in small groups	Encourage involvement in community issues	Encourage involvement with peers

Pre-Boomers	Baby Boomers	Baby Busters	Millennials
		Worship	
Authoritarian leadership	Democratic leadership	Laissez-faire leadership	
Formal oratory	Informational, conversational	Media, group-centered	Affective music
Auditory	Auditory, visual	Experiential	Experiential, visual
Silence, quietness	Talking	Talking	Talking
Hymns	Praise songs	Praise songs	Recorded and live music
Organ, piano	Guitars, drums	Jazz ensemble	Self-performed/generated music
Expository sermons	How-to sermons	Issue-oriented sermons	Narrative sermons
Pastor prays	Various people pray	Various people pray	One person prays
Guests recognized	Guests anonymous	Guests anonymous	Guests anonymous
Low audience participation	High audience participation	Low audience participation	Low audience participation
		Some Implications for the Future	
Ability to carry on programs and projects will wane	Support of people-oriented projects will continue	Involvement with issue-oriented projects/short-term mission projects will increase	Helping peers, involvement in short-term mission projects will continue
Giving will continue until retirement	Giving will be related to people projects	Giving will be related to issues, causes	Giving will be related to projects in which they are involved
Revivalist evangelism will continue to decline	Friendship evangelism will continue to be strong	Support group/12-step evangelism events will increase	Peer group sharing will continue

Table 2
GENERATION Y—THE MILLENNIALS

Generation Dates	Culture Altering Events	Period Characteristics	Societal Movements	Generational Names/Characteristics	Generational Values
1982—2002	Terrorist attacks, 9/11 a major focus	Feeling of being valued	Fear of terrorism	Generation Y	Focus on future
	Globalism	Expecting constant change	Environmental concern	Mosaics	High value on technology
	Columbine shootings	Both parents work	Smaller families in larger homes	Millennials	Borrowing to improve
	Bill Clinton sex scandals	Less anger with parents	Shift from government to self-provided retirement (see parents losing benefits)	Assumption of responsibility earlier, civic-mindedness	Experience with responsibility
	Death of dot-coms	More material benefits, more time given to children	Educational confusion, willingness to borrow to pay high costs	Goal/achievement orientation	Disbelief in instant response—TV problem solving
	Music: CDs, MTV, rap	Optimism about future		Confidence	
	Changing views on sexual freedom	Sharing of parents' work ethic	Higher optimism about future, more are educated but job market still tough	Hope/optimism	Higher purpose and drive
	Divorce and single parent families	Concern with group acceptance		Inclusiveness	More responsible gender roles
	Focus on children and family, devoted fathers	Fight to develop own cultural expressions in music and dress	Satisfaction from working with peers	Trust	Comfort with contradictions
	High value of child			Powerful influence of media, TV, digital technology	
	HIV/AIDS epidemic, other STDs	Conforming to peer pressure	Drug culture continues though heavy drug not the big problem	Acquaintance with survival realities	Enjoyment of humor
	SDA Church: Right-wing/fundamentalism onslaught	Heroism, patriotism	Multiculturalism	Feeling of being favored	Love of looks/visual dramatic entertainment
	Social narrator: Eminem	Scheduled lives	Parental advocacy	Collaboration	
				Involvement	
				Religiosity/Spirituality	

way beyond what we can discern or verbalize. There is a great distrust of any church or institution asserting that it has "the truth." Postmodernists assert that they are spiritual but not necessarily religious, that they are pro-mystery and anti-humanist.

This approach to making meaning has filtered through to the vast majority of people in the western world. Sixty-three percent of Americans believe that nothing can be known for certain except those things one experiences in one's own life.[4]

The postmodern approach to making meaning involves some or all of the following propositions:

- Things and events do not have intrinsic meaning. There is only continuous interpretation of the world.
- Continuous examination of the world requires a contextual examination; we ourselves are part of the context.
- Interpretation depends not on the external text or its author, but on the relative viewpoint and particular values of the interpreter. The interpreter becomes the final authority.
- Language is not neutral, but relative and value-laden.
- Language conveys ideology.[5]

Within this context, it is easy to see why there are so many possibilities and why everything becomes relative to the individual. When someone declares that he has "the truth," it is perceived almost as an act of violence against the freedom of all.

The World of the Postmodern Young Person

Youth today have a love/hate relationship with technology. They find it almost impossible to live without it—and with it. High tech that promised immediate connection has isolated them and left them more hungry than ever for high touch. Their education has left them skeptical about the existence of certainty. They are truly troubled by the dogmatic answer. They demand alternatives, as they have been taught that there is no such thing as absolute truth, just personal choices and preferences.

All of this has given rise to pluralism, or the preoccupation with choices. They demand that this be the case within the church, as well. They are happy to shop elsewhere if their tastes are not met, as they have choices in every other area of their lives. They often come close to proclaiming, "It's all right to believe anything so long as I believe something!"

They have a passion for building community, and in many cases their friendships have replaced their families. While they know that they cannot survive in isolation, that they need each other, they are deeply suspicious of people taking advantage of them, which keeps them in a perpetual tug-of-war: "I need you, but I can't afford to let you get too close."

An encouraging note for youth leaders and pastors is young people's renewed interest in the supernatural and the concept of mystery. They find the story of Jesus compelling and the person of Jesus very attractive. They ask questions openly and listen to spiritual alternatives, exemplifying their high level of tolerance. They are accepting of all religions and do not appreciate the vilification of any community group.

---

[1] See Neil Howe and Bill Strauss, *13th Gen: Abort, Retry, Ignore, Fail?* (New York: Vintage Books, 1993).

[2] See Neil Howe and Bill Strauss, *Millennials Rising: The Next Great Generation* (New York: Vintage Books, 2001); Lancaster, Lynn C. and David Stillman, *When Generations Collide: Who They Are, Why They Clash, How to Solve the Generation Puzzle at Work* (New York: Harper Collins, 2002).

[3] Source unknown.

[4] Sally Morgenthaler, "Out of the Box: Authentic Worship in a Postmodern Culture," *Worship Leader,* vol. 7, No. 3 (May/June 1998).

[5] Source unknown.

Chapter 6

A Simple Strategy for Reclaiming Missing Youth

I bumped into Katie on the street, and we started talking about old times. She was a singer and worship leader in her church. Not having attended her church for years, I assumed she still led out in worship there. I was saddened to learn that she had not been to church for some time.

Once a person has stopped coming to church, it takes only a matter of weeks before the old saying becomes true: "Out of sight, out of mind." The parents and immediate family are acutely aware of the loss, but no one else seems to care. Hardly a week passes that I don't receive a tearful response when I inquire about a family member:

- "He left his wife and family—and the church."
- "She finds it hard to attend church because there is no place for her female partner."
- "It's awkward with them not being married and having two kids."
- "They found it hard to come, knowing they would be talked about and criticized."
- "They tried other churches in the city—just needing a friend—and found the youth group cold and hard to break into. They just gave up!"

Each and every young person who has stopped coming to church is precious to God, as well as to the church. So, how do we avoid the "out of sight, out of mind" trap? How do we reclaim these beloved prodigals? Mentioning them in our prayers is good, but one cannot pray and then do nothing. Frederick Douglass said: "I prayed for twenty years but received no answer until I prayed with my legs."[1] Following the plan to reclaim missing young people as outlined in this chapter will put you on your knees—and give you a way to pray with your legs.

Construct a List

The first step is to find out who is still connected and who has left. The best place to start is church records; but remember, these will contain only the names of baptized youth. Another good source of names is Sabbath school record cards, which are not limited to those who have been baptized. The youth who are still attending will most likely be able to share names of young people who have slipped through the cracks. Even a simple brainstorming meeting with the youth group should uncover names. It may be difficult to connect with people who have been away from church for over five years, so you may want to limit your list to the people who have stopped coming within the past five years.[2]

Alert the Church Board

Many members will not even be aware that someone has left, and you need to make the church conscious of the loss, especially the youth leadership team. When you have secured the youth leaders' commitment to reclaiming these missing youth, alert the church board of your desire to see the return of these prodigals. You may want to talk to the board about the magnitude of the problem and provide some reasons for the young people leaving.

Pray

Most churches are blessed with prayer warriors, and these people will gladly include missing young people on the list of concerns they take to the Lord. One woman received verbal battering every time she tried to talk to her son about his tenuous connection with God. In the early hours of many mornings, he would stumble home in an intoxicated stupor and collapse into bed. As he slept, she would silently enter his room, kneel at the foot of his bed, and lift him up to God in prayer. Her persistent petitions spanning a decade saw her son return to church and take up a youth leadership role. She is still praying for the youth of her church.

Joan, another prayer warrior, posted the names of her children who had left the church up on the fridge as a constant reminder to pray for their return. She shared what she was doing with another mother in the church, who then asked if Joan would pray for her kids, as well. Other parents wanted their kids added to the list, and before long, the fridge door was too small. It was now frighteningly clear to Joan just how many of the church's children were missing. As the list continued to grow, she approached the board and asked if she could use a data projector to scroll the names on the screen between Sabbath school and church. She planned to do it only once, but it became a regular feature. It focused the congregation's prayer time, and there was real rejoicing when one of the names was removed from the list because someone had come home.

Gather Data

Gathering a few valuable details will increase your chances of a positive first contact with a missing young person. (See Appendix for a sample data collection form). On a basic level, you will need to know age and gender. Some names do not clearly indicate gender, but a chat with someone who was familiar with the young person can quickly solve the dilemma. Other basic information to obtain is a current address and phone number.

Data on the young person's family will also help in reconnecting. Are the parents married, separated, or divorced? Has one or both parents stopped coming to church? Many times a young person will stay home to support a parent who no longer attends. Also, is the young person's relationship with the family healthy, distant, hostile, or severed?

When was the last time the young person attended? The longer someone has been away, the more difficult the reclamation process is. Do any of the person's friends still attend? If so, you will want to alert them of upcoming church activities so they can invite the missing youth. Try to find out what the person had enjoyed about church, and it is important to know how they currently feel about the church. If they are angry, then you can be on your guard not to become defensive. If they are sad that no one seemed to care, then you can mount an initiative for people to visit, call, or send cards to them, and you yourself can offer reassurance that they have been missed. If they are apathetic or indifferent, then be prepared to let them know what the church is doing for its youth.

Find out if the young person is still attending school or is working full time. If in school, you may be able to reclaim them through their school friends, as many young people are greatly influenced by their social networks. If working, it may be that they decided to work on Sabbath and have stopped coming to church to avoid being a hypocrite.

The Appendix to this book is a sample form for recording your visits. Try to take brief notes of the conversations you have. Knowing what you talked about last time you met will assure the young person of your sincerity.

Reestablish Connection

Connecting with the youth can sometimes be difficult. A young pastor found it almost impossible to find the missing youth of his church. Every visit he made to their homes ended without contact. He decided to visit the worst part of town to look for them, seeking the prayer support of the church as he entered these areas every Tuesday night after prayer meeting. He visited bars, clubs, and even the red-light district. Finding himself in a basement pool hall one evening, he walked among the groups and asked for young people by name. Not having met them, he had no idea what they looked like.

At yet another group, when he mentioned a name, he caught a glimpse of a young man disappearing between the pool tables and into the darkness. Another name and another young man subtly left. When he called a third name and another young man started to move away, the pastor said, "It's you, isn't it?" He had discovered the youth from his church. Although they did not come to church, they still hung out together.

"Who wants to know?" the young man responded.

"I do."

"And who are you?"

"I'm your pastor."

"Pastor, what are you doing in here?"

"No, the question is, what are *you* doing in here? I'm here because you're here and I could never find you at home." That conversation began a friendship that deepened with time.

The pastor discovered that there was a "switchboard" in town, an elderly matriarch whom all the kids respected. She could get a message to any young person in a matter of hours. All the pastor had to do was say who he wanted to see, and they were summoned, not daring to show disrespect by not responding. The old grandmother became a vital ally in the pastor's search for his missing youth.

In our age of e-mails and text messages, it is easy to think that the best way to make connection is through electronic media. Although this is certainly a quick way to get a message to young people, it is not nearly as effective as personal contact. You need to look into their eyes as you explain how they have been missed and how much you and the church care about them.

The first meeting can be brief—10 to 20 minutes is sufficient, as you are simply reconnecting. If the person gets angry, letting you know how they feels about some of the people in the church, do not become defensive and try to correct their impressions. A simple "I am sorry that you have experienced that" will suffice. His feelings are real, and an argument will most likely just increase his sense of alienation. There will even be times when you will need to apologize on behalf of the congregation for the way they have treated them.

Continued connection is necessary, so keep up the contact. One of my deacons came to me after learning that I was doing reclaiming ministry and asked if I could visit someone for him. I readily agreed, but after learning the details, I thought I may have made a mistake. The woman had not been to church in 21 years! She was a leader of the local left-wing political party, served as a court magistrate after years of being an accountant, and was now a Pentecostal lay preacher.

She met me at the gate to her front yard. After introducing myself and my occupation, she promptly informed me of all the reasons why I should not come back. She told me why she had left the Adventist church. In her early 20s, she became the treasurer of the church and was counting the Sabbath school offering when an older member asked if she could change a large bill for him so he could give several offerings. A little later, he walked past her, could not see his large note, and jumped to the conclusion that she had pocketed it. Rumor spread through the church, and as she entered the sanctuary for worship service, she was battered with open hostility and accusation. As she walked out of the sanctuary that day, she gave the offerings and treasurer's books to the pastor, told him she was resigning, and never returned. The large bill was with the offerings.

The deacon was the only person who maintained contact, and he faithfully prayed for her for the next 21 years. I told him of my first visit, and he asked me to visit again. I did, and this time made progress from the front gate to her doorstep. Upon hearing the same story, I again apologized for the church.

I visited a third time on the deacon's insistence. This time I was invited into the living room, and she called me "pastor"—a real breakthrough. She revealed that every Sabbath for the past 21 years she had sat in that very room, worshipping God on her own. When I asked, "What is stopping you from coming back to church?" she responded, "Are those people still there?" Although my answer was "Yes," I assured her that God was doing great things in their lives.

The next Sabbath, I was in the middle of my sermon when she walked in and stood at the back. I closed my Bible and walked down the aisle while telling my congregation that one of our sisters had come home. As I hugged her, several in the congregation got up and followed my lead. There were tears and requests for forgiveness, and heaven rejoiced.

Persistent prayer and ongoing connection are vital. Even though I have told you that the best results come within the first five years, I have included this story to illustrate that you can make a difference for a missing child of God no matter how long they have been gone.

Invite to Something Neutral

Once you have reestablished contact, the time will come when you sense the person is ready to reconnect with the church. This is the time to invite them to a church activity. In my experience, people leave the church for social reasons, not doctrinal. As the person walks out, a socially focused question burns in their heart: "Do people at church really love and accept me?" The activity to which you invite them needs to begin answering this very question. I have found that prodigals do not often respond to invitations to evangelistic meetings, but will often show up at activities such as campouts, volleyball games, and roller-skating nights. A socially focused activity brings the most success because it most directly addresses the cause of their departure.

Once a person reestablishes friendships, they are more likely to be ready for less socially focused church functions. A youth camp was the entering point for Richard, the young man you met in a previous chapter. He felt comfortable being around old friends, and although we had worship twice a day, his friendships overpowered any tension and eventually ushered him into full participation. Make sure the young person's friends know of your invitation, and encourage them to give their own invitations, as well.

Some young people will jump back into church functions immediately, and others will take a long time to become fully engaged. Often, church members will need to make some adjustments as they become aware of the reasons the young person left. Being able to honestly say, "We are working to change some of the things you disliked about the church" will greatly increase success in reclaiming a prodigal.

Involve as Soon as Possible

I have visited churches that have a long, drawn out process for reconciliation. If the youth is deemed unfit for church membership, they are disfellowshipped. Should they wish to return, they can come only as far as the church entrance. After several months of this fringe acceptance, they are invited to stand at the rear of the church, later to sit, and still much later, to take a minor role at the front. It is a considerable time before they can take an active, ongoing leadership role. I find this extremely troubling.

The old adage, "Not to use is to abuse and finally to lose," overflows with relevance when reclaiming a young person. Not only does immediate involvement protect the young person's fragile new connection, it also strengthens it. Do not wait to get them involved; participation builds ownership. Richard's immediate camp maintenance responsibilities led to involvement with an evangelistic campaign, which led to his committed participation with the youth group leadership team.

Preparing the Church for the Prodigal

When the prodigal in Jesus' story turned for home, his heart longed for the father, but he was worried that his dad would not want anything to do with him. He had rehearsed his speech: "Father, I've sinned against God, I've sinned before you; I don't deserve to be called your son. Take me on as a hired hand" (Luke 15:19, Message). He did not really know his dad because "When he was still a long way off, his father saw him. His heart pounding, he ran out, embraced him, and kissed him." The son started his speech, but his father did not let him finish—he was accepted home as a son. His dad looked past the filth, ignored the stench, and he himself became dirty just with the hug. But he covered the son's filth and restored him, ordering rejoicing and a celebration party.

In Luke 15:25 (NIV) the word "meanwhile" hints that not everyone was rejoicing. The older brother, the one who never left, the one who never squandered the inheritance, despised his father's action. There was no love there, only resentment.

When I returned to the church, the door was opened wide. I discovered that the people really cared about me. They looked beyond my appearance, ignored my attitude, saw potential, and offered me opportunities to serve. Every time I share my story, someone comes to me and says, "If only my church had been like that—I may have come home years before I did. I tried several times and felt only resentment." How often this happens when our prodigal youth come home! We need to prepare the church for their return. Instead of recrimination, there should be celebration; instead of cries of self-pity, tears of joy. Often, those who refuse to rejoice are further from the Father than the prodigal. They have had all the benefits of belonging to the family, but have never chosen to really be a part of it.

Preparing the church for the homecoming is an essential element of reclamation. The worship team may need to remind the congregation that: "Since we've compiled this long and sorry record as sinners . . . and proved that we are utterly incapable of living the glorious lives God wills for us, God did it for us. Out of sheer generosity he put us in right standing with Himself. A pure gift. He got us out of the mess we're in and restored us to where he always wanted us to be. And he did it by means of Jesus Christ" (Rom. 3:23, 24, Message).

Paul exhorts us:

"If you've gotten anything at all out of following Christ, if his love has made any difference in your life, if being in a community of the Spirit means anything to you, if you have a heart, if you care—then do me a favor: Agree with each other, love each other, be deep-spirited friends. Don't push your way to the front; don't sweet-talk your way to the top. Put yourself aside, and help others get ahead. Don't be obsessed with getting your own advantage. Forget yourselves long enough to lend a helping hand" (Phil. 2:1-4, Message).

"Celebrate God all day, every day. I mean, revel in him! Make it as clear as you can to all you meet that you're on their side, working with them and not against them. Help them see that the Master is about to arrive. He could show up any minute!

"Don't fret or worry. Instead of worrying, pray. Let petitions and praises shape your worries into prayers, letting God know your concerns. Before you know it, a sense of God's wholeness, everything coming together for good, will come and settle you down. It's wonderful what happens when Christ displaces worry at the center of your life" (Phil. 4:4-7, Message).

Even though you are at home, your heart may be far from the Father. We learn from the prodigal's older brother that self-righteousness invariably leads us to misrepresent God, making us cold-hearted, critical, and unforgiving of our "weaker brothers and sisters."[3] A church that knows its own desperate need will not wish to highlight the shortcomings of a struggling son or daughter.

People often do not understand what being a Christian is all about. After the christening of his baby brother in church Jason sobbed all the way home in the back seat of the car. His father asked him three times what was wrong. Finally, the boy replied, "That preacher said he wanted us brought up in a Christian home, but I want to stay with you guys."

Another little boy was overheard praying, "Lord, if you can't make me a better boy, don't worry about it. I'm having a real good time the way I am."

As the group of Sabbath school children filed into the church service, their teacher asked them, "And why is it necessary to be quiet in church?" One bright little girl replied, "Because people are sleeping." Sadly, this view remains long after childhood for many young people. To them, church is anything but vibrant and alive, with little to no spirit of joy.

We all expect someone else to be the change agent, and so nothing changes. A mother was preparing pancakes for her sons, 5-year-old Kevin and 3-year-old Ryan. The boys began to argue over who would get the first pancake. Seeing an opportunity for a moral lesson, their mother instructed, "If Jesus were sitting here, He would say, 'Let my brother have the first pancake. I can wait.'" Kevin turned to his younger brother and said, "Ryan, you be Jesus!"

If your church is to experience the fundamental change necessary to welcome home the prodigal, everyone must stop being comfortable with someone else being Jesus.

---

[1] Cited in www.wisdomquotes.com/cat_religion.html.

[2] John S. Savage, "Ministry to Missing Members," *Leadership* (spring quarter, 1987), pp. 116-121. John Savage's research suggests that there is a good chance of reclaiming people if they are visited in the first two months of leaving, but that it becomes more difficult the longer you leave it. It will be significantly more difficult to reclaim those who severed connection two or more years ago.

[3] See Ellen G. White, *Christ's Object Lessons* (Washington, D.C.: Review and Herald Publishing Association, 1941), p. 210.

Chapter 7

Friendship, the Best Evangelism

Jesus' disciples were locked in heated debate. They wanted to know who would hold the most powerful position in His kingdom. Jesus answered their question by placing a child in the middle of the warring group and saying that their only chance of even making it into the kingdom lay in becoming like the child. Apparently, it is all about attitude, not position.

It is here that Matthew records one of Christ's most pointed rebukes: "Whoever causes one of these little ones who believe in Me to sin, it would be better for him if a millstone were hung around his neck, and he were drowned in the depth of the sea. . . . Take heed that you do not despise one of these little ones, for I say to you that in heaven their angels always see the face of My Father who is in heaven. For the Son of Man has come to save that which was lost" (Matt. 18:6, 10, 11, NKJV). It is in this context that Matthew places the parable of the lost sheep, concluding with Jesus' statement, "Even so it is not the will of your Father who is in heaven that one of these little ones should perish" (verse 14).

It is clear that Jesus desires His disciples to search for lost sheep, who in this context are the children of the church. There are many obstacles we must fight against in order to do this. There may even be times when the church actively discourages you from seeking these missing young people.

> If you are pursuing lost sheep, you must go where they are. You cannot avoid every appearance of evil. Our Lord didn't, either. Because of His close proximity to the beer cans and potato chips of His day, He was accused of being a drunkard and a glutton. Professional "weaker brothers," suffering from hardening of the categories, delight to criticize those who take the Great Commission seriously.[1]

Our model for reclaiming ministry is found in the life and work of Jesus. He called himself the Good Shepherd, who Himself left a place of safety to search out the lost. As His method centered on the incarnation, with Him becoming one of us, our ministry for lost youth is to be "incarnational." What does this mean?

To incarnate Jesus in this world, the Christian must experience an inner transformation in which he not only behaves as Jesus behaved, but also shares His love, His valuing of persons, His compassion, and His zeal for justice and righteousness. This character, stamped indelibly on his heart and mind, will be read by all men (2 Cor. 3:2). The incarnation of Jesus in the LAOS [people] of God is to be an incarnation of God's love in personal relationships.[2]

Youth ministry built on this model seeks to meet young people where they are and to offer them pastoral care, relating to them not only as spiritual guides, but also as counselors and friends—fellow pilgrims on a similar spiritual journey. With Jesus as our model, we are called to a personal and relational ministry that will involve a good deal of one-on-one time. Pete Ward, the London University Youth Ministry professor, spells out just what incarnational ministry will involve:

Youth work that is incarnational will see in the life of Jesus a model for ministry. It is essential, not only to good practice, but also to the proclamation of the gospel, that relationships are at the heart of the work. Dean Borgman says that we are called to "waste time" with young people "hanging out" with them. Unprogrammed social time will form the heart of our ministry as it seems to have done in the life of Jesus. Young people will learn to become Christian because they are in regular informal contact with Christian people who model the faith. The dilemmas and challenges of Christian discipleship will be dealt with as we are on the move from one informal activity to another—car journeys, conversations while going fishing, coffee in the kitchen, a postcard sent from a trip abroad. The substance of incarnational ministry is the valuing of contact between adults and young people in the everyday and ordinary things of life. Friendship and relationship will not only be the means of ministry, they will be the ministry itself.[3]

Ellen White, decades ahead of her time, encouraged incarnational ministry with young people. She made it clear that we must enter into the feeling of the youth, working with them in their joys and sorrows, their conflicts and victories. She said that we must meet them where they are if we are to stand a chance of keeping them. It is easy to misjudge them because of the way they dress or speak, but we need to spend time with them, building relationships. We need to get to know them.[4]

One young person made the following statement, spelling out the necessity of the church connecting with him. "Practically, for the church to welcome me, it needs to honor the truth I bring with me, welcome my energy, and bless my inexperience. For me, there is nothing more discouraging and soul-sucking than entering a church and leaving without anyone saying hello, showing interest in me, or inviting me to be involved."[5]

Once relationship is established, the story of Jesus seen in your life becomes that much more compelling. Kevin Graham Ford tells us that teenagers are drawn by the magnetism of Jesus. He says they "are very open to the Christian story right now—if it is presented in an effective and appropriate way. They may be closed to old, outmoded evangelistic methods, but not to the story itself."[6]

The old adage, "I'd rather see a sermon than hear one any day!" is especially true for teenagers today. They find it difficult to see the story of Jesus behind a screen of inconsistency, and a caring connection will cut through that screen. They want to see Jesus lived out in your life. He needs to be far more than just a part of history or part of a good argument; He needs to be real, living, present. One young person described it this way:

> My generation demands a different apologetic—an embodied apologetic, a flesh-and-blood, living and breathing argument for God. The old apologetics of previous generations assumed that the barrier to conversion was intellectual and the way to remove that barrier was to answer all cognitive doubts. But Xers live in an age of intellectual ambiguity, when cognitive answers carry considerably less weight. The question my generation asks is not "Can Christians prove what they believe?" but "Can Christians live what they believe?"[7]

Active Listening

How many times have you heard a young person say, "You never listen to me," or, "You never seem to hear what I have to say." Young people are hungry to be heard, and given the opportunity, they will share quickly and easily. Listening to a young person is the quickest way to build a relationship. And it will be the relationship that draws them closer to God and allows them to see Jesus in you.

I believe Scott Peck had it right when he wrote:

> The principle form that the work of love takes is attention. When we love another, we give him or her our attention; we attend to that person's growth.... When we attend to someone, we are caring for that person. ...You cannot truly listen to anyone and do anything else at the same time.... True listening, total concentration on the other, is always a manifestation of love. An essential part of listening is the discipline of bracketing, the temporary giving up or setting aside of one's own prejudices, frames of reference, and desires, so as to experience as far as possible the speaker's world from the inside, stepping into his or her shoes. The greatest gift that you can give anyone is your complete attention.... True listening is love in action.[8]

Harry Stack Sullivan propounded the idea that all personal growth and healing are developed through our relationships with others. He suggests that what we are at any given moment in the process of becoming a person is determined by the relationships we develop with other people.[9]

Dr. Paul Tournier gives insight into humanity's need for connection:

> How beautiful, how grand and liberating this experience is, when people learn to help each other. It is impossible to overemphasize the immense need humans have to be really listened to, to be taken seriously, to be understood. Modern psychology has brought it very much to our attention. At the very heart of all psychotherapy is this type of relationship in which one can tell everything, just as a little child will tell all to his mother. No one can develop freely in this world and find a full life without feeling understood by at least one person.[10]

The Five Levels of Communication

John Powell describes five levels of communication. Understanding these levels will increase the efficiency and meaning of the communication between you and the young person to whom you are ministering. With practice, you can help them to understand themselves more deeply and to more efficiently communicate their discoveries, which will strengthen the bond between you. You may observe several of these levels in one conversation, and don't be surprised if the second level surfaces early.

Level 5—Small Talk

At this level, shallow conversation takes place. "How are you?" "What's up?" "How's it going?" Such conversation borders on the meaningless, as it is mostly clichés, but it can sometimes be better than awkward silence. When communication remains on this level, it is boring and leads to frustration and resentment in relationships.

Level 4—Factual Conversation

At this level, information is shared, but with no personal comments. You tell what has happened, but do not reveal how you feel about it. Males are more apt to settle for this level than females, as they are often less able to express their feelings.

Level 3—Ideas and Opinions

Real closeness begins here, for on this level you risk exposing your own thoughts, feelings, and opinions. Because you feel free to express yourself and verbalize personal ideas, the young person has a better chance to know the real you and trust deepens. Sharing becomes more meaningful, and the door is opened for the young person to share more openly with you. Don't try to start at this level; there is a process that you must work through to arrive here.

Level 2—Feelings and Emotions

Communication at this level describes what is going on inside you—how you feel about someone else or a situation. You may verbalize feelings of frustration, anger, resentment, or happiness. Sharing honestly in a give-and-take manner and showing interest in the young person's feelings and in expressing your own will enrich your relationship. You will both feel noticed, valued, and loved. You will receive flashes of insight into their character that will greatly increase your understanding of how they really think and feel. Try alternating between ideas/opinions and feelings/emotions to increase conversation meaning even more.

Level 1—Deep Insight

Rare moments of profound insight will occur when you are really in tune with another person in understanding, depth, and emotional satisfaction. Communication of peak experiences and other deeply personal issues makes deep impressions on both parties, enriching the relationship. This is the pinnacle of human communication, and you will not—nor are you supposed to—experience this level with everyone. It occurs most often in marriage relationships or in very close friendships.[11]

Common Communication Spoilers

Since most of us have a strong desire for effective communication, why is it so rare and difficult to establish? One of the prime reasons is that people unknowingly inject communication spoilers into their conversations. These barriers can soak up an astounding 90 percent, or more, of meaningful communication time, especially in conversations in which one or both parties has a problem to be dealt with or an unfulfilled need.

Communication spoilers are high-risk responses that frequently, though not inevitably, impact communication negatively. These roadblocks are more likely to be destructive when one or both parties is under stress. The unfortunate effects of communication barriers are many and varied: They frequently diminish the other's self-esteem; tend to trigger defensiveness, resistance, and resentment; can lead to dependency, withdrawal, and feelings of defeat or inadequacy; and decrease the likelihood that the other will find their own solution to their problem. Each spoiler is a "feeling-blocker," reducing the likelihood that the other will constructively express their true feelings. Because communication spoilers carry a high risk of fostering these negative results, their repeated use can cause permanent damage to a relationship.

What specific spoilers are apt to hinder a conversation? Interpersonal communication experts have pinpointed responses that tend to block communication. More recently, Thomas Gordon devised a comprehensive list that he calls the "dirty dozen" of communication spoilers.[12] These 12 barriers can be divided into three major categories: "judgment," "sending solutions," and "avoidance of the other's concerns."

The first four fall in the "judgment" category:

Criticizing

This barrier shows up when one person communicates a negative evaluation of the other's person, actions, or attitudes. "You brought it on yourself—you've got nobody but yourself to blame for the mess you're in."

Name-calling

This is putting down or stereotyping the other person. "What a dope!" "Just like a woman." "You hard hats are all alike." "You are just another insensitive male."

Diagnosing

This occurs when one person plays amateur psychiatrist and guesses why a person is behaving as they are. "I can read you like a book. You are just doing that to irritate me." "Just because you went to college, you think you're better than I am."

Praising Evaluatively

This barrier appears when a positive judgment of the other person, their actions, or attitudes, is made. "You are always such a good girl; I know you will help me with the lawn tonight." Teacher to teenage student: "You are a great poet!" (Yes, praise can indeed be a high-risk response.)

The next five spoilers are categorized as "sending solutions," which especially hinder communication for the young person who simply wants someone to listen.

Ordering

This is to command the other person to do what you want to have done. "Do your homework right now." "Why?" "Because I said so."

Threatening

This barrier shows up when one person tries to control the other's actions by threatening negative consequences. "You'll do it or else . . ." "Stop that noise right now or I will . . ."

Moralizing

Put simply, this is "preaching" at someone. "You shouldn't get a divorce—think of what will happen to the children." "You ought to tell him you're sorry."

Excessive/Inappropriate Questioning

Excessive questioning is a common barrier and makes the young person feel like they are being interrogated. "When did it happen?" "Are you sorry you did it?"

Advising

A person brings this into play when they tell the other person what course of action they should follow. "If I were you, I'd sure tell him off." "That's an easy one to solve. First . . ."

The last three communication spoilers are often perceived by youth as tricks to avoid their real concerns.

Diverting

When a person pushes the other's problems aside through distraction, they are diverting. "Don't dwell on it. Let's talk about something more pleasant." Or, "Think you've got it bad? Let me tell you what happened to me . . ."

Logical Argument

This is attempting to convince the other with an appeal to facts or logic, usually without consideration of the emotional factors involved. "Look at the facts: if you hadn't bought that new car, you could have had your college fees instead."

Reassuring

Reassuring is an attempt to stop the other person from feeling the negative emotions they are experiencing. "Don't worry. It is always darkest before the dawn." "It will all work out in the end."

Basic Attending Skills

Attending skills are basic to empathy, the ability to experience and understand the world of another human being. A person with good attending skills is proficient at focusing on the other person and their point of view.

Faulty listening is at the root of most communication problems. Sometimes it merely causes annoyance or irritation. But when a person is trying to get a problem resolved, or is seeking emotional support, poor listening can have disastrous results.

God created us with two ears and one mouth. Maybe that should give us a hint as to how much we should use each one. Yet most of us prefer to talk rather than listen. We enjoy expressing our ideas and telling what we know and how we feel. We expend more energy in expressing our own thoughts than in giving full attention when others are expressing theirs. Listening seems like such a simple thing to do, yet most of us are poor listeners because listening is hard work.

Effective Listening Methods

Emphasis on effective listening is not new, but until recently, the ability and willingness to speak freely has been a more popular topic. Today, corporations encourage employees to take listening skills courses, and family counselors emphasize the importance of listening within the family circle. Following are some techniques suggested by a collection of experts to help you enhance your listening abilities.

Be alert to body language.

We communicate by the spoken word, but we also communicate by what we do not say. Facial expressions make up 55 percent of what we communicate: a pout, a sigh, a grimace, a squint of the eyes. Such body language speaks louder than words. We send other nonverbal messages through body postures or gestures: a nervous tapping of the foot, tightly clenched teeth, a motion of irritation. Nonverbal communication hints at true feelings and sets up barriers before conversation even begins.

Open the door.

A "door opener" is an effective listening technique that does not convey any of your own thoughts or feelings, but merely opens the door for the young person to say more. Some simple door openers are: "I see," "You don't say," "Tell me more," "I'd be interested in your point of view," or "Tell me the whole story." Instead of getting the impression that you can hardly wait to snatch the conversation away, the young person feels respected and hears, "I am genuinely interested in what you have to say," "I can learn something from you," and "Your ideas are important to me."

Listen actively.

Deliberate listening is the ability to process information, analyze it, recall it at a later time, and draw conclusions from it, but active listening hears the feelings of the speaker first and then processes information. Both deliberate and active listening skills are necessary in effective communication, but listening with feeling is far more important to growing relationships.

Active listening is particularly useful when you sense the young person has a problem, such as anger, resentment, loneliness, discouragement, frustration, or hurt. Your first reaction to the facts you hear may be negative; you may want to argue, defend yourself, fight back, or withdraw. But to listen actively, you purposefully strain out the facts and restate the feelings you heard expressed.

Some Simple Rules for Effective Listening

Perhaps you have been a poor listener and want a change. Merely deciding to "listen harder" will not work. You must discipline yourself and make a firm commitment to improve this skill. Here are six ways you can become a more effective listener:

Maintain steady eye contact.
Focus your full attention on the speaker.

Sit attentively.
For a few minutes, decide that nothing else in the world matters except hearing the young person out. Block all other distractions from your mind, and lean forward in your chair.

Prove your attentiveness nonverbally.
Raise your eyebrows, nod your head, smile, or laugh when appropriate.

Prove your attentiveness through appropriate phrases.
Sprinkle your attentive listening with appropriate phrases to show agreement, interest, and understanding. The young person wants to know that you understand the ideas they are presenting. Try to think through their words and fit them into your own experience.

Ask well-phrased questions.
Give encouragement by asking questions that illustrate your interest.

Listen a little longer.

Just when you think you are through listening, listen 30 seconds longer—you may be surprised at how much more you learn

Feedback

Feedback is information communicated to someone about the quality of their interaction with others. It enables them to adjust their behavior to better achieve their goals.

Each person interprets the words and actions of others in the light of their own background, experience, attitudes, need satisfaction, values, etc. Because of the complexity and variety of these factors from person to person, intentions are often misinterpreted. When a young person misinterprets our intentions, the only way to become aware of their resulting negative feelings is for them to communicate them. Guessing is extremely inaccurate because their feelings are uniquely theirs and live deep within them, beyond our command. Their feedback gives us the opportunity to change our behavior and more accurately communicate our intentions. Without it, we will likely continue our behavior, they will likely continue their misinterpretation, and their negative feelings will grow, impeding communication more and more.

For example, a young person may be trying to gain acceptance by the church youth group, but the group is rejecting them because of the way they are going about it. The young person redoubles their efforts, which only accelerates the rejection. The process gets locked tighter and tighter in a circular pattern until someone cares enough to give the young person feedback about how their behavior is negatively affecting the group. They can then adjust their behavior, increasing their chance for success.

Affirmations

We tell people how we expect them to behave and feel about themselves by what we say to them and about them. Affirmations are powerful, positive, verbal, or nonverbal messages that define who we are and how we expect to be treated. Other people can give them to us, or we can give them to ourselves.

The following affirmations are messages that invite others and ourselves to become whole, capable people who care about themselves and others. The following apply to varying age groups[13] and are especially relevant for youth.

Affirmations for Being
"You have every right to be here."
"Your needs are OK with me."
"I'm glad you are who you are."
"I'm glad you're here."

Affirmations for Doing
"You don't have to do tricks to get approval."
"It's OK to do things and get support at the same time."
"Try things, initiate things, be curious, be intuitive."
"I'm glad that you're here, and I see that you're doing things."

Affirmations for Thinking (It's OK to Think)
"I'm glad that you're growing up."
"I'm not afraid of your anger."
"You can think about what you feel."

Affirmations for Identity (Learning Who You Are)
"You can be powerful and still have needs."
"You can express your feelings directly."
"You don't have to act scary, sick, sad, or angry to have your needs addressed."

Affirmations for Structure (Learning to Do Things Your Own Way)
"You can do it your way."
"It's OK to disagree."
"You can think before you make that rule your own."

Affirmations for Spirituality
"You can reach out to God."
"You can have doubts."
"It's OK to grow."
"You can think, decide, and act according to your faith."

A young person's self-image sets the boundaries for their psychological and spiritual growth. The healthier their self-image, the more they will achieve. Belonging, worth, and confidence make up our self-image. Belonging comes from our relationships, worth from what we are, confidence from what we can do. In addition to belonging, youth need recognition and affirmation for who they are, not just for what they do.

If we are to woo young people back to the church, we are going to have to get serious about it. It will cost us time and energy and may call for some appreciable individual and corporate changes. When the shepherd Jesus told us about walked out into the dark night to find the lost sheep, it was at great personal risk.

If we are going to model our approach on that of Jesus, we will recognize that reclaiming ministry cannot be effective at a distance. To minister to youth, we must be accessible to them. Further, Lawrence O. Richards asserts that the youth minister must in fact become one of them.[14]

It is not enough to read about the youth's subculture. One must intentionally place oneself in the midst of it, coming close enough to touch and be touched. To get so close is to be vulnerable, possibly to be hurt or even crucified.[15] Reclaiming ministry requires and enables us to stand in the thick of it, between God and people, sacrificing to bring the two together. Young people desperately need to see Christ, and they will see Him and His sacrifice in you and yours.

Jesus appointed youth, our neighbors, to be the recipients of our ministry and to profit from our gifts. Christ's solidarity with humanity is such that, as we minister, we minister to Him. When we go into the world of youth, we meet Him there.[16]

The incarnation brought God within our reach and made Him understandable. Jesus was God's clearest statement about Himself. The challenge of reclaiming youth lies in translating God's revelation and reconciliation into language that they can clearly understand. This requires the translators to understand the culture of those to whom they minister, and they can achieve this only by following Jesus' footsteps into the heart of it, enabling the gospel to be heard, seen, internalized, and applied right where young people are.

Clearly, when we remain detached from the world of the youth, our ministry is weakened and may be totally ineffectual. Ray Anderson makes this comment: "The church that denies its solidarity with the world becomes an untruthful church and no longer has the incarnational credibility that is the mark of Christ Himself. . . . The solidarity of kenotic community acts as a living context in which the Christian closes the circle of transcendence by living as Christ in the world."[17]

Jesus accepted people; He loved them without condition. The youth minister will woo and win young people as they offer them unconditional love and acceptance. Jesus built enduring friendships as He shared trust and belief in people, drawing them by His open and caring spirit. Youth ministry will succeed only as it is built on His highly relational model.

> In a culture like ours, where the individual is so dehumanized, the recovery of genuine humanity begins with the forming of real friendships. Friends genuinely care for one another. A friend does not "use" the other person to achieve some goal.... Friends trust each other. Friendship transports a person from concern for self to concern for another. Friends are willing to "bear one another's burdens."[18]

[1] Joseph Aldrich, "You Are a Message," *Moody Monthly*, 1982, cited by Doug Stevens, *Called to Care* (Grand Rapids, Mich.: Zondervan, 1985), p. 119.

[2] Lawrence O. Richards and Martin Gib, *A Theology of Personal Ministry* (Grand Rapids, Mich.: Zondervan, 1981), p. 101.

[3] Pete Ward, *God at the Mall: Youth Ministry That Meets Kids Where They're At* (Peabody, Mass.: Hendrickson, 1999), pp. 37, 38.

[4] Ellen G. White, *Gospel Workers* (Washington, D.C.: Review and Herald Publishing Association, 1948), pp. 207-212.

[5] Jarrett Kerbel in Gary Zustiak, *The Next Generation: Understanding and Meeting the Needs of Generation X* (Joplin, Mo.: College Press Publishing Company, 1996), p. 165.

[6] Kevin Graham Ford, *Jesus For a New Generation: Putting the Gospel in the Language of Xers* (Downers Grove: Intervarsity Press, 1995), p. 173.

[7] *Ibid.*, p. 174.

[8] M. Scott Peck, *The Road Less Traveled: A New Psychology of Love, Traditional Values, and Spiritual Growth* (London: Arrow Books, 1993), pp. 135, 136.

[9] John Powell, *Why Am I Afraid to Tell You Who I Am?* (Hong Kong: Fontana/Collins, 1990), p. 43.

[10] Paul Tournier in John Powell, p. 5.

[11] Material based on John Powell, pp. 54-62.

[12] Adapted from Thomas Gordon, *Parent Effectiveness Training: The "No-lose" Program for Raising Responsible Children* (New York: Peter H. Wyden, 1970), pp. 44, 108, cited in Robert Bolton, *People Skills* (Sydney: Simon and Schuster, 1987), chapter 2.

[13] Barry Gane, *Building Youth Ministry: A Foundational Guide* (Riverside, Calif.: La Sierra University Press, 1997), p. 121.

[14] Lawrence O. Richards, *Youth Ministry: Its Renewal in the Local Church* (Grand Rapids, Mich.: Zondervan, 1979), p. 25.

[15] Doug Stevens, *Called to Care*, p. 27.

[16] Thomas F. Torrance, "Service in Jesus Christ," *Theological Foundations*, p. 723, states: "Hence Christ is to be found wherever there is sickness and hunger or thirst or nakedness or

imprisonment, for He has stationed Himself in the concrete actualities of human life where the bonds and structures of existence break down under the onslaught of disease and want, sin and guilt, death and judgment, in order that He may serve man in re-creating his relation to God and realizing his response to divine mercy." J. S. Whale, *Christian Doctrine* (Cambridge: The University Press, 1956), pp. 145, 146, cited by Keith Miller, *Habitation of Dragons* (London: Word, 1970), p. 39, says: "Faith without ethical consequences is a lie. Good works must necessarily follow faith. God does not need our sacrifices, but He has, nevertheless, appointed a representative to receive them, namely our neighbour. The neighbour always represents the invisible Christ."

[17] Ray S. Anderson, "Living in the World," *Theological Foundations for Ministry* (Edinburgh: T. & T. Clark, 1979), pp. 591, 592.

[18] William Mahedy and Janet Bernardi, *A Generation Alone* (Downers Grove: Intervarsity, 1994), p. 80.

Chapter 8

Church Climate and Youth Ministry

If we are going to get serious in attempting to stop the hemorrhaging of the church, we must start by caring for the youth we already have. A good place to begin is to learn their names.

Much of the research into how kids survive in difficult situations and continue to function revolves around the concept of resilience. How do they get resilience? From us. "We surround them with social support or a loving and caring environment, we learn their names and greet them personally, taking a few moments to talk one-to-one, and we develop enduring relationships with them. Through these steps they build strength and improve their ability to defeat overwhelming odds they face every single day."[1] We cannot overstate the power of the presence of a caring adult in the life of a young person, someone who consistently cares for and supports them through good and bad times.

Results from the Valuegenesis study support the concept that caring adults can effectively reach kids through the youth ministry program of the local church. It is clear that those kids involved in a strong youth ministry program do better in many areas of their lives than do others.[2] Youth who have relationships with caring adults in the context of youth ministry programming have much higher levels of mature faith than do their counterparts.

Among the many scales developed in the Valuegenesis study was the "mature faith" scale, measuring both vertically (relationship to God) and horizontally (social concern). Among other things, this scale revealed that only 42 percent of youth with no access to youth ministry reported that they seek opportunities for spiritual growth, while 69 percent of those in the strongest youth ministry programs sought these opportunities. Where youth have little or no youth ministry, only 20 percent tell us that they care a great deal about reducing poverty, while 40 percent of those in active youth programs feel strongly about it. These results were consistent for all the items in the "mature faith" scale.

"Intrinsic orientation to religion" is the term that G. W. Allport used to describe the internalization of religion.[3] In his studies he found that intrinsic orientation to religion among teenagers is a strong predictor of deep religious conviction in their adult years. Youth with higher levels of intrinsic orientation to their religion are far more likely to remain in the church.

As we examine individual items within the "Intrinsic Orientation Scale," we find that only 28 percent of those without youth ministry see private prayer and devotion as important to them, as opposed to 50 percent of those involved with a youth program. Only 8 percent of those without youth ministry enjoyed reading about their religion, while 27 percent in strong youth ministry programs found this activity enjoyable. Does religion answer questions about the meaning of life? Seventeen percent of young people without a youth ministry answered yes, while for those with a youth ministry program exactly twice that percentage responded affirmatively.

Of the young people in the Valuegenesis study who were not involved in a youth program, 61 percent told us that they intended to remain involved in the church when they turned 40. Significantly more of those involved in a youth program answered affirmatively (85 percent). Involvement in a meaningful youth ministry also seemed to predict greater satisfaction with the church.

One surprising finding in the study regarded the perceived influence of the pastor in the development of faith. Where there is a weak or no youth ministry program, only 45 percent perceived the pastor as having significant influence, whereas 72 percent of those in a strong program thought so.[4]

Figures 1 and 2 reveal the significant disparity in youth perceptions and attitudes in churches with and without youth ministry. When youth ministry is offered more than once a week, 71 percent attending those churches reported going to church because they want to, compared with only 39 percent attending churches without such a program. Sixty-three percent look forward to going to church where there is regular youth ministry, and where there is none, that number falls to 23 percent. The disparity between the two groups is just as marked for the other items (see Figure 1).

A youth program also influences young people's perceptions as to whether the church is open, warm, flexible, and exciting. Youth with a weekly youth ministry program are more inclined to see their church as growing than are those without it. We also find that young people in

Figure 1. Youth Ministry and the Local Church (Valuegenesis II)

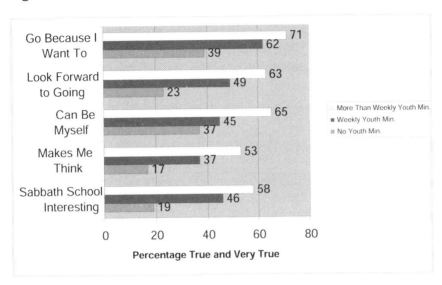

Figure 2. Impact of Youth Ministry on Perceptions of the Church

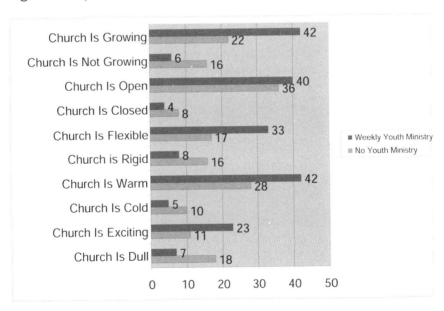

churches with meaningful youth ministry programs are much more likely to see their church as welcoming to strangers; however, the opposite is true for those without it. Overall, youth involved in meaningful youth ministry programs are much more likely to perceive the church climate as healthy.

There is also a difference in youth perception related to the church's thinking climate. Where there is a strong youth ministry program, 55 percent of respondents felt challenged to think (as opposed to 27 percent), 52 percent felt they were being stretched in worship (as opposed to 28 percent), and 48 percent felt they were encouraged to ask questions (as opposed to 26 percent).

One of the things that causes concern for parents and youth leaders is the youth penchant for experimentation. It appears that a large number of youth in any faith community will experiment with various "at-risk" behaviors. Junkin suggests from her research and experience that youth leaders, and to some extent, parents:

> . . . should recognize and be supportive of this time of questioning and exploration. Truly listening to students and hearing their concerns rather than telling them what they should do and be fosters growth instead of further rebellion at this stage. Thoughtfully provoking appropriate answers and creating an environment where students feel free to openly question without guilt, provides valuable opportunities to encourage final commitments that augment adolescents' recognition of God's will for their lives.[5]

Junkin further states that "Christian educators, pastors, and youth workers are in the unique position of assisting adolescents in developing a healthy, well-integrated, personal and spiritual identity."[6] A. W. Litchfield[7] found that future-intended religious participation influenced involvement in deviant behaviors even more than current religiosity, and knowing that adolescents involved with youth ministry are more likely to have positive intentions regarding future involvement in the church should strengthen our resolve to facilitate youth ministry.

The Valuegenesis research examined involvement in at-risk behavior. The survey instrument asked how often in the last month teens had used alcohol, tobacco, marijuana, or cocaine, been binge drinking,[8] been violent, shoplifted, or been in trouble at school. It also asked about sexual activities, depression, and thoughts of suicide. There were major differences in the behavior of the youth depending on their level of involvement in meaningful youth ministry. In the sample with meaningful youth ministry, 79 percent had not used alcohol, as opposed to 66 percent without. Ten percent fewer of those with youth ministry reported binge drinking and tobacco use, 6 percent fewer reported having had sexual intercourse in the past month, and fewer suffered depression and suicide attempts. The Australia/New Zealand Valuegenesis[9] study found major differences in youth attitudes toward the church's position on these at-risk behaviors (see Table 1). The local churches were used to gain our sample of youth, rather than the church school system.

Table 1
Attitudes of Adventist Youth to Traditional Adventist Behavioral Expectations

	Youth Ministry	No Youth Ministry
One should not use tobacco (p<.05)	89%	56%
One should not drink alcohol (p<.05)	82	50
One should not listen to heavy rock music (p<.05)	46	22
One should not dance (p<.05)	16	11
One should not use illegal drugs (p<.05)	90	72
Sex should occur only within marriage (p<.05)	74	45
One should not eat unclean meat (p<.05)	70	45
One should not use caffeinated drinks (p<.05)	27	17

The evidence is overwhelming. If you wish to close the back door of the church, you must have a strong youth ministry program—one that offers variety in worship experiences, opportunities to lead, and challenges that cause youth to think through the important issues of faith and community. Youth ministry is not an option; it is an imperative.

Recalling the reasons young people gave for severing connection with the church will give us an indication of what will need to change if we stand a chance of bringing them back for good. Adults can admit that their lives do not always reflect what they preach. They can be more open to sharing how God has worked in their lives, as well as more open about still having progress to make.

When challenged by young people that they are focusing on unimportant issues, church leaders should listen and even be prepared to adjust their focus. How important is the format of services? By how much do the advantages of an unbending dress code outweigh the disadvantages?

Tony Campolo tells the story of a very conservative and highly structured church that had a young, disheveled, long-haired, dirty visitor enter midway through the service. As he walked down the aisle, the end of each row was occupied and no one looked like moving along to accommodate him. He kept moving toward the front, and now with every eye watching him, he wished he had not walked in and disturbed things. Finally, finding himself directly beneath the pulpit, he saw no option but to sit down on the carpet. The congregation was relieved to see an old, well-groomed member stand and move forward with the help of his ornate walking stick. Surely the young lout would be asked to leave. As the old man arrived, he steadied himself with his cane and then quietly sat down on the floor beside the young man. What a wonderful sermon to see!

Older members may not think that they are critical and uncaring, but innocent remarks can often be misunderstood. If older members concentrate on the positive and ignore the negative, the youth will grow in maturity.

Margaret, one of the finest church leaders with whom I have had the privilege of working, was well into her 80s when the church asked her to take greater leadership responsibilities. They saw the way she worked with the children and youth and the peace that resulted. When a young person contributed in any way to the church, she would always thank them and send them a card or note to let them know how much they were appreciated. She never missed a birthday or major event in any of the young people's lives. She let them know that she would be praying for them as they undertook examinations or job interviews. She loved and was loved, and now having passed away, has left a sparkling legacy in the lives of hundreds of young people.

When young people express an impression that the church is preoccupied with organization and not concerned for people, we face a great challenge. If the leaders of the church and a good number of older members can just learn and use the names of the young people, they will begin to alter this impression. Open discussion with the youth as to their needs and the types of ministry, worship, and programs they want to see will also adjust this perception. When genuine ministry is happening, this perception begins to fade.

Of growing concern are the progressive approaches to worship that are being introduced. In some churches, we have witnessed worship wars, leaving some congregations almost destroyed. Usually, this is not about change for change's sake, but an attempt to make worship a little more relevant and meaningful. While change can be good, if too many changes are introduced all at once, the church may become unsettled and make the older members feel insecure. This is an area that will take a lot of open discussion, negotiation, and time.

It took two years and many church business meetings for my home church's leadership team to allow change. We began with youth-led worship services once every three months. Young people invited their friends from school and work, and they appreciated the new approach to worship so much that by the end of the year they wanted to lead out once a month. After a few years, we went to weekly youth-led services, and attendance swelled from the normal 25 to a regular 400. The more contemporary service is held in the church hall because it seats twice as many as the church. Approximately one third of the adults accepted an invitation to support the youth service, and the rest remained in the main sanctuary. Interestingly, the numbers in the main sanctuary have not changed much for over 10 years, but the youth church has now outgrown the accommodation, and the church is set to expand to a new site. The church has learned to accept and appreciate the enthusiastic approach the younger generation brings to worship. Thank God for a group of adults who have learned to be tolerant, open, caring, and visionary!

The following quote from aging rock star Boy George is an insightful example of the way church is often perceived:

> On Sunday I attended the christening of my year-old godson Michael, and he was as restless as everyone else. The priest was a lovely man with impeccable dress sense, but I was confused from the moment he took the pulpit. . . . What's the point of rattling on about sin when most of us are doomed to eternal damnation? It doesn't warm people to Christianity, it only makes them feel like hypocrites. Worse still are the utterly depressing hymns. I'd like to see live music, acoustic guitars, and percus-

sion. Church should be a joyous and liberating experience—[it] badly needs a face-lift because it is God's theatre on earth, and He should be packing them in.[10]

Those young people who tell us they don't come to church because they don't want to be hypocritical can be supported by a group of adult leaders who share some of their own struggles and who really know the grace of God in their lives.

It is hard to find anyone who can't remember feeling that the church was restrictive when they were young. I have found that when youth are involved in service projects or ministry endeavors, the sense of being restricted tends to fade. When you don't have any ownership of church ministry, you feel restricted because many of the alternative ways to spend your time cut across what is appropriate for young Christians. When the church is interested in both the social and spiritual aspects of kids' lives, it will work to engage them in lots of fun, growth-inducing activities. This takes time and demands attention, but it pays dividends. Many of the youth who have come to my church for its social side have stayed on to become vital parts of its worship and ministry.

A truly active youth ministry that caters to fellowship, nurture, worship, and outreach will offer an attractive alternative for those who are tempted to try a different lifestyle. If they are surrounded by friends, pull-away will be much weaker. When youth take responsible leadership roles in fellowship and fun activities, nurture and growth initiatives, worship in all its aspects, and mission and evangelism, they will be thought leaders, and we will not hear the complaint, The church does not allow me to think for myself. Times of open discussion when the youth are encouraged and feel safe to explore alternative ideas will do much to strengthen their relationship to the church community.

The following points may be helpful in getting these discussion times started:

Ask questions that are more open than closed.

These are questions that begin with who, what, where, when, and why. They cannot be answered with only a yes, a no, or a grunt.

Ask only one question at a time.

Because we can find silence awkward, we often ask another question before the youth have time to think about a response.

Present questions to the whole group.

Youth do not like to be singled out and put on the spot, and this is easily avoided by seeking discussion from the whole group.

Provide feedback after a group member responds.

Even if you don't appreciate and/or disagree with a response, acknowledging the response with feedback is important because it affirms the young person and encourages further participation.

After an initial question and response, follow up with probing questions.

This needs to be done in an inquiring tone that genuinely seeks to better understand the response.

After asking a question, be silent.

Learn to live with silence. If you sit there and wait, then the youth will realize you are really serious about hearing from them. Just a rephrasing of the question may be necessary if you think they really did not understand.

Use an inquiry—not an interrogation—style.

Encourage group members to ask their own questions.

Getting kids to think, inquire, and propose ideas will encourage them to take greater leadership roles, and will equip them for those roles.

Avoid echoing group member response.

Truly reflecting on what a young person has said is not to simply parrot their response. A thoughtful summary will let them know that you have heard and are serious about understanding their input.

Accept group member responses as if they were gifts.

Anyone who has worked with kids for any length of time is aware of how challenging it can be to lead a meaningful discussion. When you do get a response, build on it by affirming and thanking them, and then tease out a little more interaction.

---

[1] Gary L. Hopkins and Joyce W. Hopp, *It Takes a Church: Every Member's Guide to Keeping Young People Safe and Saved* (Nampa, Idaho: Pacific Press Publishing Association, 2002), 43.

See also R. Brooks, "Children at Risk: Fostering Resilience and Hope," *American Journal of Orthopsychiatry* 64, No. 4: pp. 545-553.

[2] Barry Gane and Jimmy Kijai, "The Relationship Between Faith Maturity, Intrinsic and Extrinsic Orientation to Religion, and Youth Ministry Involvement," *The Journal of Youth Ministry* 4, No. 2 (2006); pp. 49-64

[3] G. W. Allport, *The Individual and His Religion* (New York: Macmillan, 1950).

[4] If the pastor has multiple churches, some with youth ministry and some without, the youth in the churches with youth ministry are far more likely to see the pastor as influencing their growth in faith.

[5] M. Junkin, "Identity Development in the Context of the Faith Community," *Christian Education Journal* 6 (2000), p. 38.

[6] *Ibid.,* p. 40.

[7] A. W. Litchfield, D. L. Thomas, and B. D. Li, "Dimensions of Religiosity as Mediators of the Relations between Parenting and Adolescent Deviant Behavior," *Journal of Adolescent Research* 12 (1997): pp. 199-226.

[8] Binge drinking is regarded as having five alcoholic drinks in quick succession.

[9] A. Barry Gane, *Youth Ministry and the Transmission of Beliefs and Values.*

[10] Boy George, *London's Daily Mail* (February 23, 2000), cited in Jonathan McKee, *Do They Run When They See You Coming?* (Grand Rapids, Mich.: Zondervan, 2004), pp. 45, 46.

Chapter 9

Missing Body Parts

When a young person turns their back and walks away, the Lord is deeply hurt. I imagine it is like having a limb severed from His body. Paul likens the church to the body of Christ five separate times.[1] In 1 Corinthians 12 he offers the following description of the church: "For we were all baptized by one Spirit into one body—whether Jews or Greeks, slave or free—and we were all given the one Spirit to drink. . . . Now you are the body of Christ, and each one of you is a part of it" (verses 13, 27, NIV).

My memories of church reach back to my early childhood. The church my family attended was a very small, inner-city building crammed between two factory blocks. Its external walls and roof were made of corrugated iron, making it perfect for roasting in the summer, freezing in the winter, and going deaf during the frequent rainstorms. We traveled an hour each way to get to the church.

My younger sister and I were the only kids in the church. We fought all week long, so my mother separated us on Sabbath, one on either side of her in the back row. This location made for an easy exit when we got out of hand, which was close to all the time.

My 20-something father, who worked extremely long hours during the week, usually leaving and coming home while I was still in bed, had been the church elder from the time of my birth. He was also the Sabbath school leader, the treasurer, and most weeks, the deacon. Since we could not afford family vacations, the only time I got to see this hero in my life was on Sabbath—but then he was up front most of the time. You might think this would make me resent church, but I loved it! The people made the difference.

Each week, one of the older members would arrive late and go through an elaborate routine before finally being seated. He would hook his umbrella over the back of the pew in front of him, drape his black overcoat next to it, and perch his bowler hat on the end of the pew. He would greet the little lady who always sat next to him, preen his whiskers (which rivaled those of Santa Claus), and settle in for the duration. I would look at my sister, and she at me, and we would almost choke trying to hold back the laughter. But we did not want to be taken out yet—we knew there was more to come!

Within minutes of the sermon starting, his breathing would get heavier, and shortly after, the snoring would start. Gentle at first, it would soon crescendo into a roaring sound. His head would drift to the side and settle on the shoulder of his little seatmate, and she would sink further down into the pew. When she could stand it no longer, her hand would fly up to adjust her hat, from which she would withdraw an enormous hat pin. With some ceremony and surprising energy, the pin was plunged deep into the snoring giant's posterior. He would wake with a yelp, straighten with a start, and be terribly alert for a very short period of time.

My sister and I would not yet give in to the comedy of it all—because there was still more to come! As he drifted back into the snoring pattern, something in his mind would not let him slump over on the lady again, and he would invariably fall off the end of the pew in the opposite direction, landing startled and very apologetic in the aisle. I can't tell you what happened next because by this time my sister and I had lost control and the fit of giggles could not be contained.

Space does not permit me to introduce all the members of my childhood church, but I want to say something about them as a whole. Being the only two children in the church meant that we were loved and spoiled. They never tired of us and were interested in our young lives. We were deeply loved, and we knew it!

When we think of "church," many of us picture a building. But the church is not just bricks and mortar, roof, walls, and windows. It is easy to look at the church as a place where you go once a week, rather than the gathering together of the body of Christ to worship God. Acts 16 tells us that the church gathered by a riverside. Paul speaks of the church meeting in the home of Aquila and Priscilla. When we see that the church is people—that it is you and me—then things change. We begin to understand that we need each other, that we are dependent on each other. We see that the church's intended influence is diminished when a young person disconnects.

Paul makes it clear that each person brings the gifts of God to the church, offering something different but equally important. "The body is a unit, though it is made up of many parts; and though all its parts are many, they form one body. So it is with Christ" (1 Cor. 12:12, NIV). Each person brings a different gift "so that the body of Christ may be built up" (Eph. 4:12). It is easy to look at someone else's outstanding contribution, feel inferior, and think, I have nothing to offer. Paul addressed this: "If the foot should say, 'Because I am not a hand, I do not belong to the body,' it would not for that reason cease to be part of the body" (1 Cor. 12:15).

Have you ever done repairs on your car? Have you wriggled underneath to tighten bolts or remove a part? Have you felt the frustration of finally arriving at the spot, having left the skin of your elbows on the ground and that of your nose on the undercarriage, only to realize that you have not brought the right tool with you? What a relief to see a pair of feet approach and hear a voice ask, "Do you need a hand?" The hand that brings you the right tool for the job is very important, but that hand is connected to an arm that is just as important. And that arm is connected to a shoulder that moves it around, and on and on, eventually leading back to the brain that controls it all. Although the hand gets top billing, it would be nothing without its teammates.

Paul is saying, Don't diminish yourself, don't put yourself down. You are of value and the body of Christ needs you as much as you need your own feet. "If the whole body were an eye, where would the sense of hearing be? If the whole body were an ear, where would the sense of smell be?" (1 Cor. 12:17, NIV).

In our weakness sometimes the members of the body diminish the value of other members. As a young pastor I was given a small country church in a regional town in England. The town had 144,000 residents (a significant number), and it was my goal to have all of them as members of my church. I began by visiting all the people on the church roll.

One morning, I found myself outside the Barkers' house. I did not know anything about them and already had in my mind what they could do to bring the gospel to their street. A glance through the window began to adjust my expectations—they were clearly elderly. I gently knocked on the door and no one answered. I saw a big brass doorknocker and used it with vigor. Still no response. And then I saw the doorbell. The window to the front room was only feet from the door, and so with my finger on the doorbell, I leaned over to look in the window. As I pressed the doorbell, the lights flashed on in the house. Press doorbell, lights flash. Press doorbell again, lights flash again. Wow!

I was off-balance and feeling like a kid with his hand in the cookie jar when the door opened. I straightened up and said very quickly, "Hello, I'm Barry Gane. I'm your new pastor, and I just came by to see how you are doing." The lady's expression remained unchanged, making me wonder if she'd heard me, so I repeated my speech. This time I tried to enunciate more clearly, but soon became conscious that she was intently watching my mouth. Not remembering if I had brushed my teeth, I tried to cover them with my lips. She interrupted me and said, "I'm sorry young man, but I'm deaf and I am trying to read your lips and you seem to have a strong accent." When I was finally able to communicate who I was, she invited me in.

As I entered the front room, there was an elderly man sitting in a chair. I greeted him, but there was no response. Assuming he was hard of hearing, I shouted my greeting, only to have Mrs. Barker tap me on the arm and gently inform me that her husband was deaf, did not speak, and had also lost his sight.

The visit was difficult. Every letter of every word I said was traced onto the man's hand. I had been there only a few minutes, but it seemed like ages. Thinking the best thing would be for me to beat a hasty exit, I offered to pray. As I asked for a blessing on their home, I opened just one eye to secretly catch a glimpse of the translation process. Tears coursed down the wrinkled cheeks. I found out later that no one visited—everyone found it too difficult.

As I left the place, to my shame, I said to God, "You sent me to this town to capture it for you, and I have a whole slew of old people who can't do anything. The people I just met are both deaf and the husband is blind, as well. What good are they?"

Duty pressed me, and so I visited on a regular basis and was soon adopted by the elderly couple. I would always leave feeling they had given me so much more than I had given them.

When spring came, I asked if Mr. Barker would like to go for a walk.

What a mistake! It took forever with him leaning on my arm just to get to the front door. But after we were on the street, he started to walk more quickly. After only a short time, he stopped and I thought, "Good, he's tired and we can head back home." He then embarrassed me by waving his hand in the air. I instinctively asked what was going on, only to remember that he couldn't hear me. Looking up, I realized he was reaching for a branch he knew had to be there. He had not always been blind and his nose told him exactly where we were. The double cherry blossom was in bloom and I had walked past without noticing it. I gently pulled the branch down and he smelled it, brushed it against his face and then took my hand and spelled out the word b–e–a–u–t–i–f–u–l. The elderly man had once again ministered to his pastor.

"If they were all one part, where would the body be? . . . The eye cannot say to the hand, 'I don't need you!' And the head cannot say to the feet, 'I don't need you!'" (1 Cor. 12:19, 21, NIV). Paul goes on to say that we all have different functions, and that we are all necessary to make the body whole. Jesus considers each member of His body as equally important, but do the members of His body share this mind-set? Can you imagine what it must be like for Jesus at times? He has a plan but he can't get his feet to move. His hands refuse to reach out to touch and His arms to hold. His body flails awkwardly much of the time, not cooperating with His intentions.

By 6 months of age it was clear that Christy Brown faced a number of challenges. Doctors announced that he would not be able to walk, talk, or even brush his teeth. He would be forever dependent on someone else's care. They strongly encouraged his mother to put him in an institution where professionals could tend to his severe needs. But she loved the boy, he belonged to her, and she refused to give up on him.

It was difficult and extremely time-consuming, but as she constantly read to him, talked to him, and explained things to him, she was convinced that there was something going on inside his head, even though there was no apparent response. She found a doctor who said that the drug he was experimenting with might give Christy control of just his neck muscles, enabling him to nod his head. It was a small step, but it increased his ability to communicate.

Christy's mother developed an attachment that she strapped to his forehead. Sitting him in front of a typewriter, she said, "Christy, talk to mom." It took an age as Christie concentrated and struggled, but eventually, there it was: "I love you, Mom!" Over the ensuing years, those four simple words evolved into widely read, prize-winning poetry and short stories. Here was an important little boy locked inside a twisted, writhing body that he could not control. Every single person had given up on him—except one loving parent who was willing to be a part of Christ's body working in harmony with His intentions.

When leprosy attacks the body's nerves, the leper can turn a key but not know when it is finished turning. He may keep turning until the key snaps or the skin on his fingers breaks open. Paul wants us to know that when the body is functioning well, not only does it do the bidding of Jesus, but it is aware of the needs of every part: ". . . there should be no division in the body . . . its parts should have equal concern for each other. If one part suffers, every part suffers with it; if one part is honored, every part rejoices with it" (1 Cor. 12:25, 26, NIV).

One can to a large degree take the temperature of the body by observing how the individual members treat each other. When a young person returns to church, will they find it welcoming and warm, and will the other members of the body accept them, rejoicing that they are home again? Or will the church refuse the hand that may have once been dirty or used to bring disgrace?

It was through the church that Jesus offered the world the greatest evidence of His existence and His intentions toward it. "By this all men will know that you are my disciples, if you love one another!" (John 13:35, NIV). "We know that we have passed from death to life, because we love our brothers. . . . This is how we know what love is: Jesus Christ laid down his life for us. And we ought to lay down our lives for our brothers" (1 John 3:14, 16, NIV).

> Lord, we are your body,
> Make us an instrument of your peace.
> Where there is hatred, let us show love,
> Where there is injury, let us show pardon,
> Where there is doubt, let us show faith,
> Where there is despair, let us show hope,
> Where there is darkness, let us show light,
> And where there is sadness, let us show joy.

O Divine Master,
Grant that we may not so much
Seek to be consoled as to console,
To be understood as to understand,
To be loved, as to love;
For it is in pardoning that we are pardoned and
It is in accepting your death that we bring life.
Amen.[2]

---

[1] Rom. 12:5; 1 Cor. 12:12-27; Eph. 4:4, 12; Col. 1:24.
[2] This is a play on Saint Francis of Assisi's famous prayer for peace.

Chapter 10

Why Are They Like That?

I was running a weekend retreat for teenagers in one of the churches in my district. Because this church had the most young people on its roll, all the youth in the district were invited to assemble there for the weekend. When I arrived, I was surprised to find that there were no youth there. I was informed that none of the local youth would be coming because none of them came to church anymore.

I was particularly looking forward to seeing Graham. I knew he was struggling with church and thought that this weekend would be a great way to ease that tension through reconnecting with his friends. He made a grand entrance on his motorcyle by popping a wheelie in the parking lot. As he parked the bike, a deacon met him and told him in no uncertain terms that he was not welcome and that he should leave.

As I talked to parents, I learned what had caused the disintegration of the youth group. The deacon who had just asked my boy to leave had sometime before discovered that there was a missing hymnbook and believed that the youth club was responsible. He and the elder demanded that the youth club be closed and that further youth activities be closely monitored.

I asked the deacon what had happened with Graham, and he replied that the church was better off without his type and that he had told him to beat it. "Men never do evil so completely and cheerfully as when they do it from religious conviction."[1] It was all I could do to remain cool. Asking him about the missing youth from his church, his words revealed his lack of concern: "They knew the truth, and if they decided to leave, that was their decision." They had been told, and according to him, he was not responsible for their decision. I immediately thought of the older brother in Jesus' story of the runaway youth. He stayed at home all right, but he lacked compassion for his young brother, unveiling a joyless experience and a tenuous connection with the Father in the process.

Many people believe that all we have to do is tell young people "the truth," which releases us from further responsibility. They don't think we need to make the church attractive or even do anything that would encourage them to be involved. They forget Ellen White's comment:

> There must be more study given to the problem of how to deal with the youth, more earnest prayer for the wisdom that is needed in dealing with minds. . . . We should seek to enter into the feelings of the youth, sympathizing with them in their joys and sorrows, their conflicts and victories. . . . We must meet them where they are if we would keep them. . . . Let us remember the claim of God upon us to make the path to heaven bright and attractive.[2]

Many church members show the attitude that young people should "sit down and shut up" until they are 30, that there is no place for involvement—and definitely not leadership.

The theology driving this mentality is built on a few isolated texts, such as Luke 9:62, where Jesus said, "No procrastination. No backward looks. You can't put God's kingdom off till tomorrow. Seize the day" (Message). And He appeared to give limited opportunities to those who turn aside in Matthew 10:14, when He said, "If anyone will not welcome you or listen to your words, shake the dust off your feet when you leave that home or town" (NIV). A few of Jesus' parables suggest that we get only one chance, and if we say no, it is our own fault and we will pay the penalty. The wedding garment of Matthew 22 is an example.

These instances need to be balanced with the stories of the lost sheep, the lost coin, and the lost boy in Luke 15, in which Jesus encourages us to search diligently and not to give up in our efforts to bring the lost home. In 1 Corinthians 3 Paul outlines a process in which a number of people worked with individuals before they came to a decision. He said that he planted, Apollos watered, and God caused the gospel to find acceptance and grow. We know from Jesus' story of the workers (Matt. 20:1-16) that there will be those who will make a last-minute decision and still receive the same reward. Also, Jesus didn't give up on Peter, even when Peter denied any connection with Him, not once, not twice, but three times!

The gospel is all about grace—unmerited, undeserved favor. "But God demonstrates his own love for us in this: While we were still sinners, Christ died for us, . . . When we were God's enemies, we were reconciled to him through the death of his Son" (Romans 5:8, 10, NIV). When Peter, in his ostensible generosity, suggested that he should forgive someone seven times, Jesus quickly corrected him and multiplied Peter's boundary by 70, implying that God's grace is limitless (see Matthew 18:22).

Jesus gave us an imperative to go and find the lost sheep, search for the lost coin, and welcome home the runaway. His descriptions of the resulting celebrations in the earthly settings revealed what happens in heaven: "There is rejoicing in the presence of the angels of God over one sinner who repents" (Luke 15:10, NIV).

This is a little story about four people named Everybody, Somebody, Anybody, and Nobody. There was an important job to be done and Everybody was sure that Somebody would do it. Anybody could have done it, but Nobody did it. Somebody got angry about that because it was Everybody's job. Everybody thought that Anybody could do it, but Nobody realized that Everybody wouldn't do it. It ended up that Everybody blamed Somebody when Nobody did what Anybody could have done.[3]

Let me challenge you to be that somebody who extends the gift of grace and widens the path to welcome God's sons and daughters home. Don't leave it to anybody just because everybody should do something. Be the person who welcomes the runaway and teaches the church to celebrate when a precious person comes home. Chap Clark says this about preparing to meet the needs of youth:

The "how" is not nearly so important as the "who" in creating a welcoming place for the person who seeks to know Christ and commit to the church. I am convinced that kids are not so much concerned about the kind of programs we offer as they are concerned that they fit, that they matter, and that they are important players in the grand scheme of life. Any number of models and programs with a missional commitment can accomplish this, and every model I know can fail miserably, too.[4]

If we are going to succeed, we must be intentional about connecting with and asserting that the church is a home for all youth.

---

[1] Blaise Pascal.

[2] Ellen G. White, *Gospel Workers*, pp. 208-212.

[3] Source unknown.

[4] Mark H. Senter III, Wesley Black, Chap Clark, and Malan Nel, *Four Views of Youth Ministry and the Church* (Grand Rapids, Mich.: Zondervan Publishing House, 2001), p. 110.

FRIENDSHIP RECORD BLANK

Name_____ Age_____ Gender_____

Address_____

City_____ State_____ Zip_____

Phone: Cell_____ Home_____

Baptized? Yes ❑   No ❑   Date last attended_____

Parents: Married ❑ Separated ❑ Divorced ❑   SDA? Yes ❑   No ❑

Friends still attending:_____

_____

_____

What he/she enjoyed about church:_____

_____

Present relationship with church:_____

Present relationship with family:_____

Works only? ❑   School only? ❑   Both? ❑

Dates of visits:

First_____ Second_____ Third_____

Fourth_____ Fifth_____ Sixth_____

Comments:_____

_____

_____